KATHERINE BERNHARDT

HOUSES

Dedicated to Julie Taubman

BIKING IN THE DUNES.
SOLAR ECLIPSE AND
DOUBLE DIAMONDS

KATHERINE BERNHARDT

While painting at a residency in the Elaine de Kooning House in the Northwest Harbor, Khalifa and I decided to go discover the Dunes. Brendan Dugan invited us over to go swimming in his house which is located in the Dunes. We had never been there before. We noticed he had bikes. Biking is freedom. We decided to check out the hood. I went off first by myself and happened to run into Phil and Sarah from CANADA while walking home from the beach. They were staying at a friend's home in the Dunes. I got to see that house too. I rode back to the pool excited about the cool architecture I had just discovered. Now Khalifa and I decided to ride around. Brendan had also pointed out a Geller House near his that had just been restored. I also noticed the house from *The Affair* was in the Dunes as well. Thus began my obsession or interest with houses in the Dunes and the architecture of the Hamptons. Andrew Geller in particular.

We started biking a lot to and from the pool to the beach, everyday looking at the amazing beach architecture in the Dunes. We went on a field trip one day to West Hampton to visit the *Double Diamond* house by Geller. The Solar Eclipse also happened to be that same day, so we saw the Geller house and the Solar Eclipse in the same time frame.

Back at the Dunes we discovered huge and small wonderful wood and glass masterpieces, some with crazy window shapes, some A-frames, some with concrete, all interesting designs. It was exciting to ride bikes and take pictures at the same time… trying to take pictures with one hand while riding a bike.

Later on at the de Kooning house I decided to make black ink drawings of the houses I had seen and of the house I was staying in. The de Kooning house resembles a spaceship and is elevated above the ground and has a wrap around porch that you can view the forest from. So I started making fast black ink sumi-e like drawings of the houses, breaking down the houses to their basic forms of line. They became like Japanese calligraphy quick line drawings.

We also took another field trip to visit a Geller house that was for sale in Sag Harbour. The house had been restored, a window added, and the wood had been painted and the character taken out of it. Someone also added a pool and a pool house and the place was set on five acres of land for sale. The house was A-framed.

We were invited to dinner at *The Affair* house, which is also an Andrew Geller beach home. A friend of a friend owns it and we had the pleasure of being invited and eating a delicious seafood soup there. The interior was all wood and kept intact. I noticed there was a painting on the wall of a house that was from down the street of one of the other best houses in the neighborhood, with a cool round concrete entrance. Seeing that painting also sparked my interest in making my own drawings of houses.

I had never really spent any time in the Hamptons before, so it was eye-opening for me to see all this amazing architecture. It is also such a foreign idea to me that people actually live in houses and have tons of space and live so remotely. Staying in the de Kooning house was terrifying at first having so much space and so many doors to lock and to stay safe from "monsters." But we got used to it. It was such a luxury having so much space to work. I made all the drawings at the kitchen table where Elaine de Kooning used to work as well. It was such a neat atmosphere to stay in this house and paint and be in the woods, working in total isolation in the woods.

Biking in the Dunes was inspirational, shirt and clothes off. Swimsuit on, crocs on, sandy toes and wet hair. Huge open wide blue sky and the smell of pine trees. Dark green pines against a blue sky. Beautiful. Fresh Air.

Elaine de Kooning House, Northwest Harbor

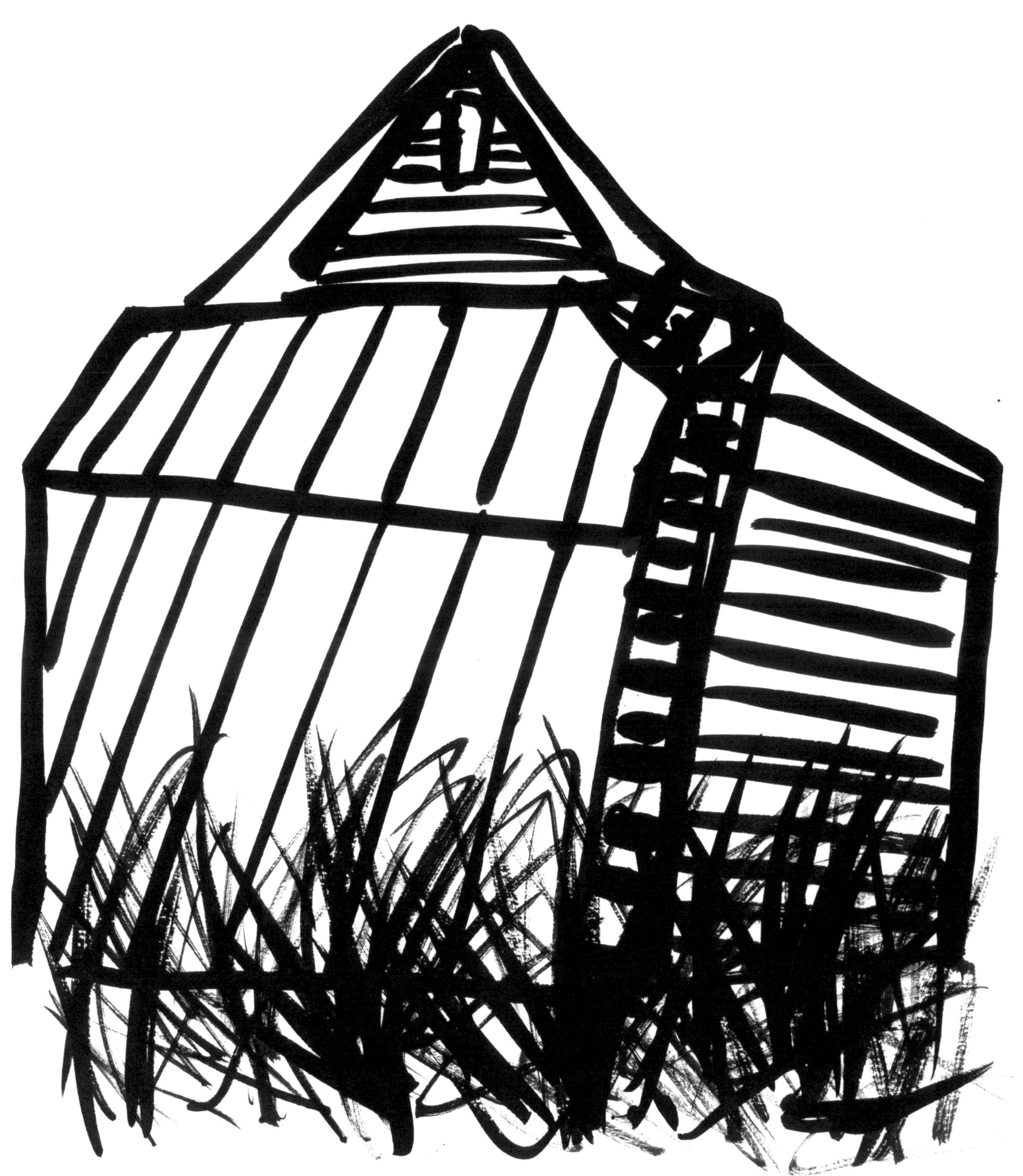

Elaine de Kooning House, Northwest Harbor

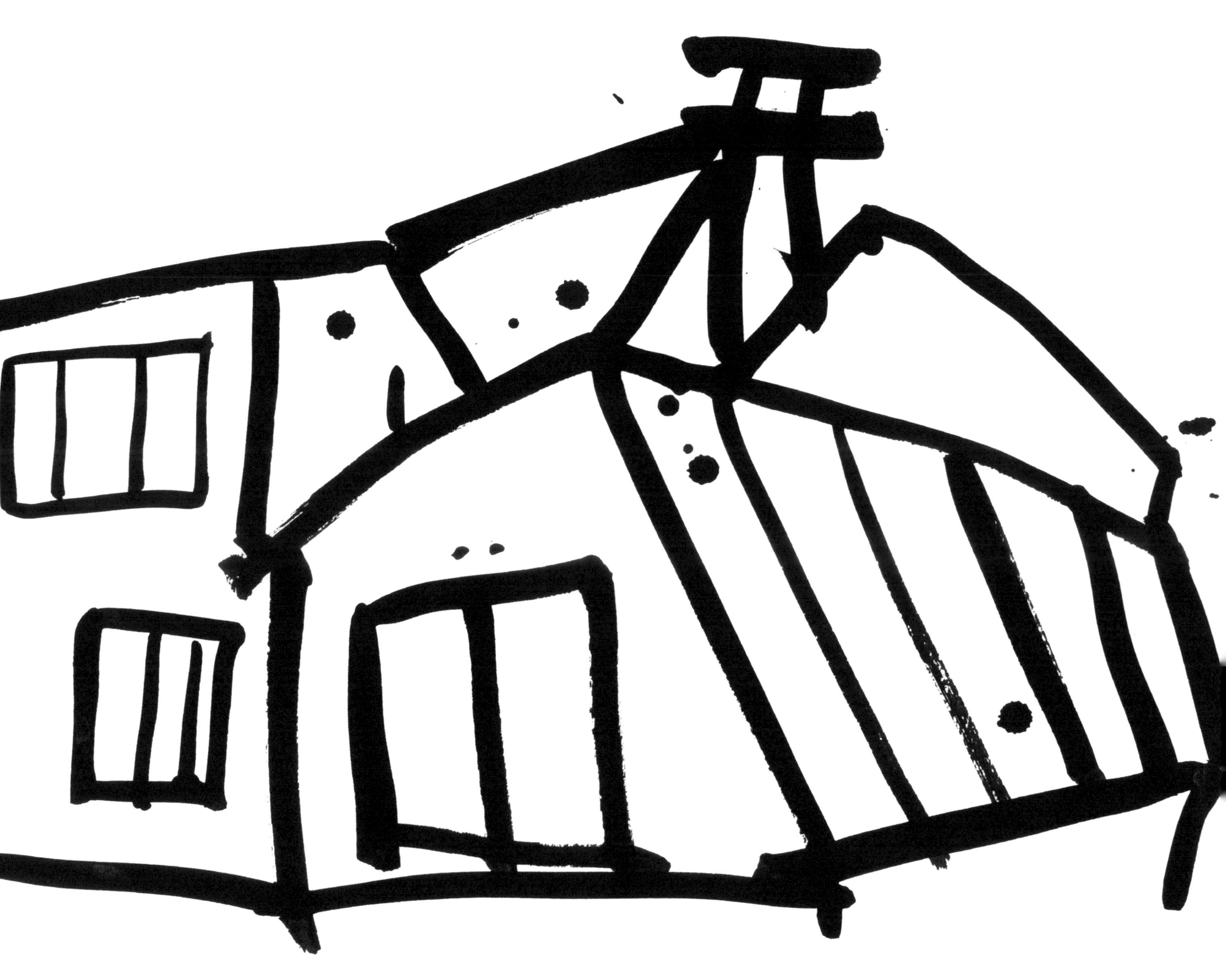

Sag Harbor

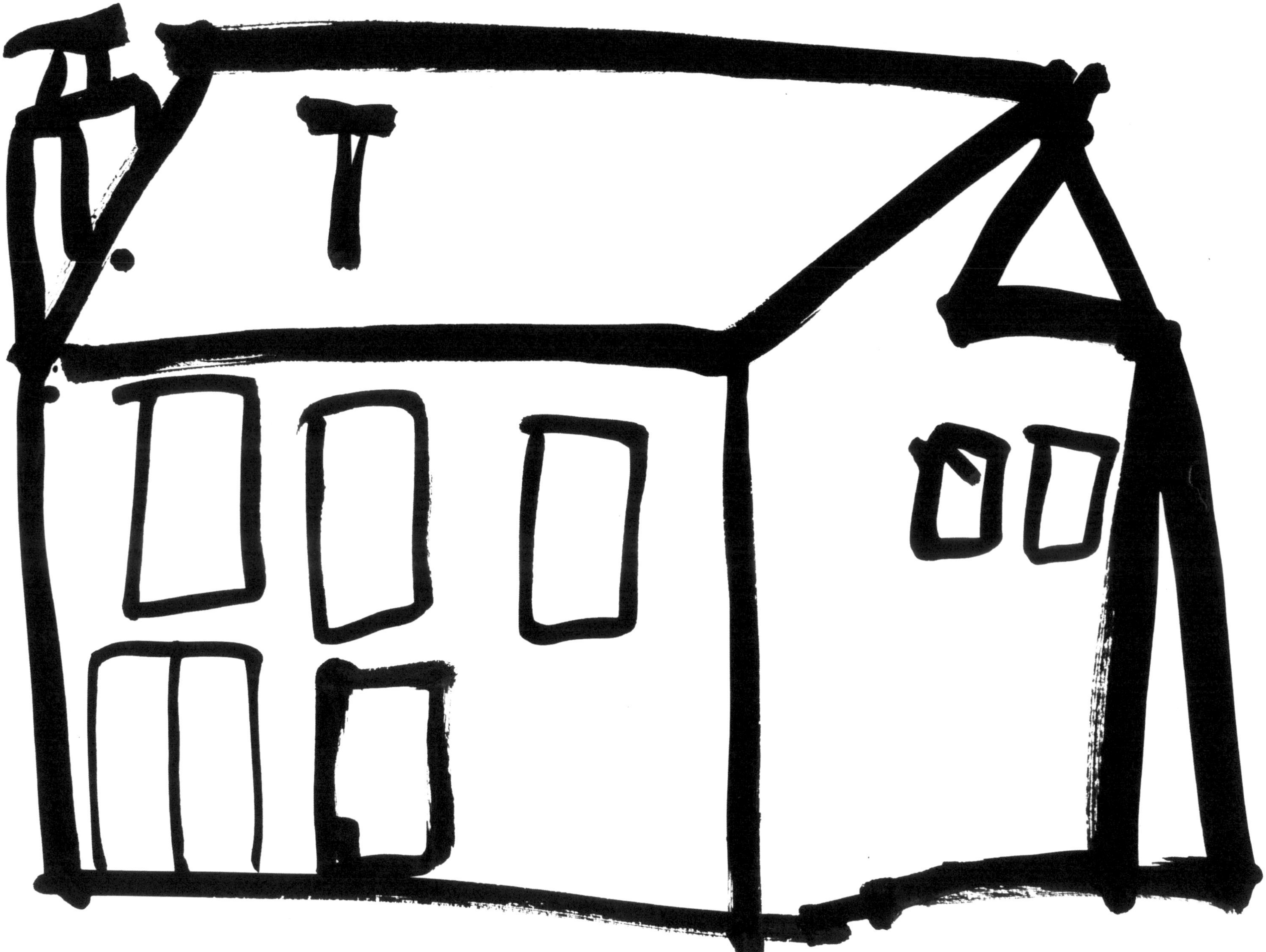

Northwest Harbor

Elaine de Kooning House, Northwest Harbor

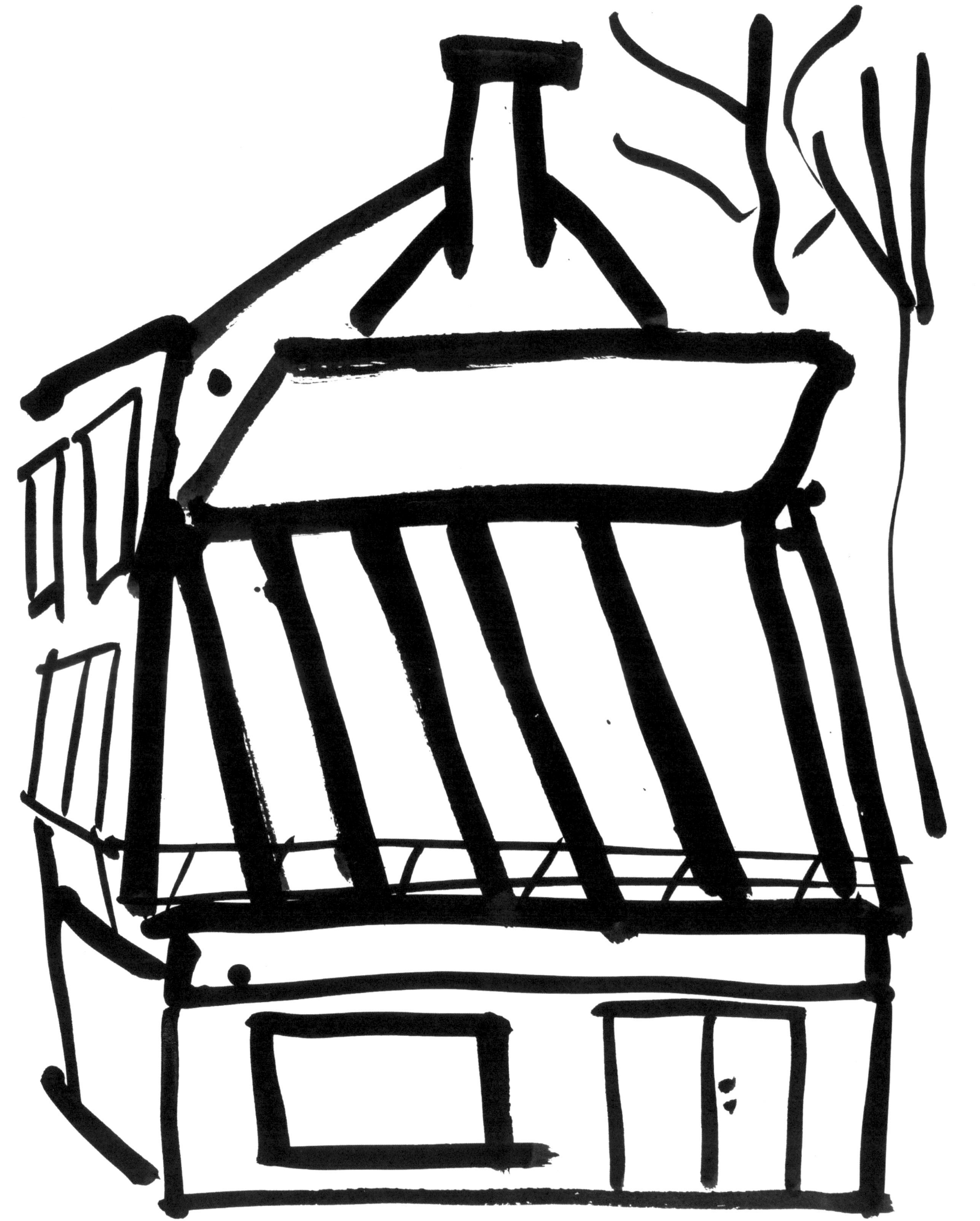

Elaine de Kooning House, Northwest Harbor

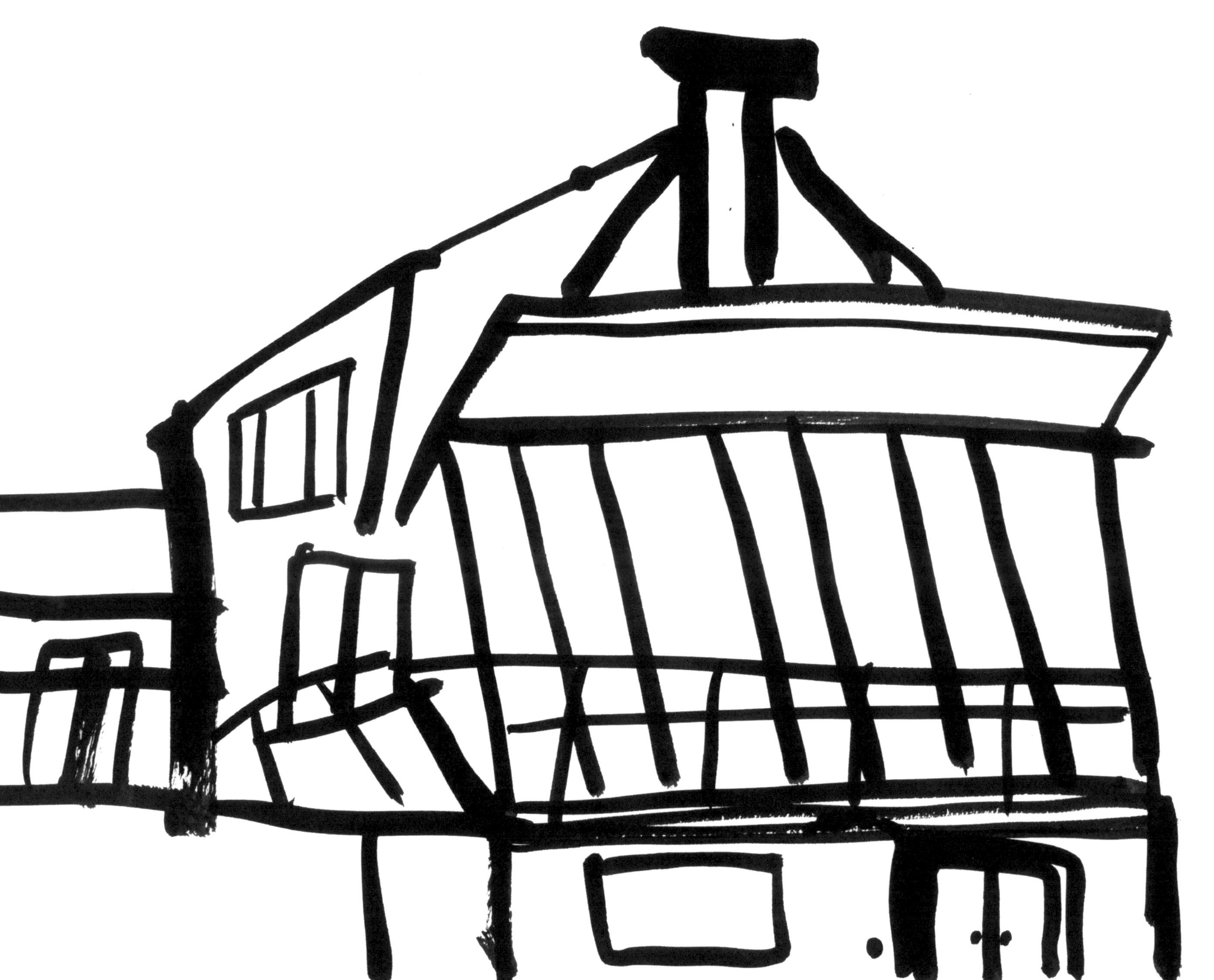

Northwest Harbor

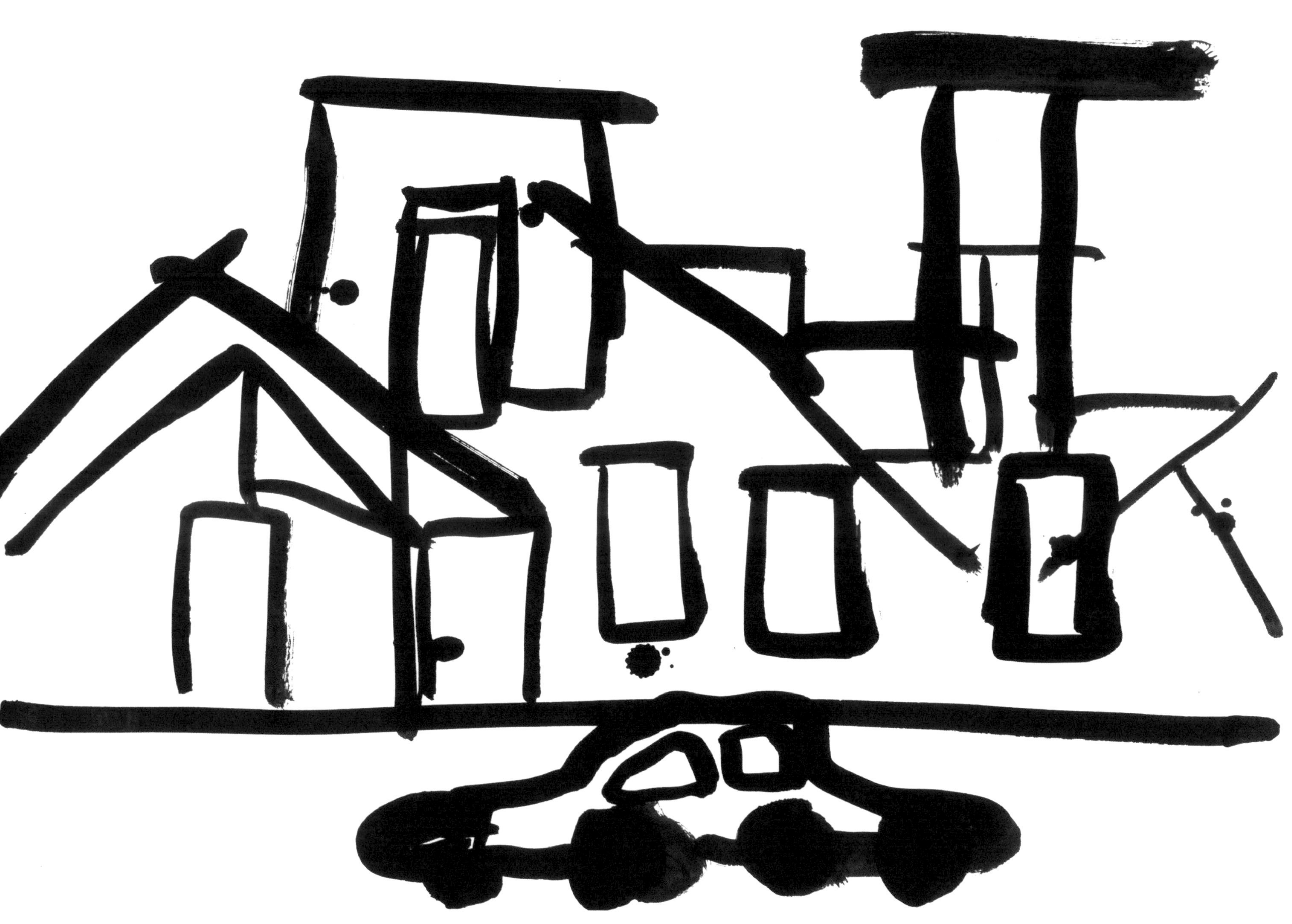

Dunes

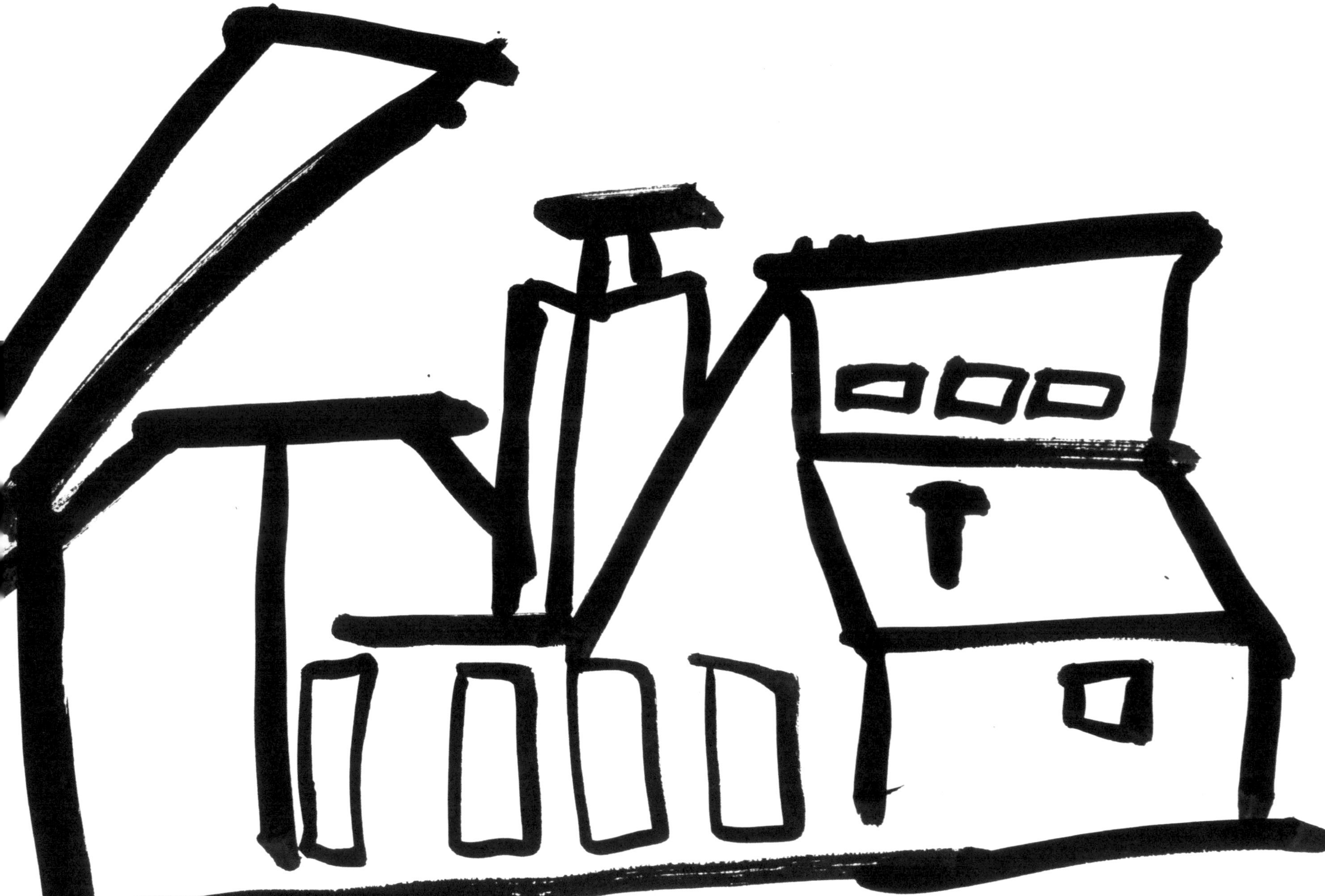

Dunes

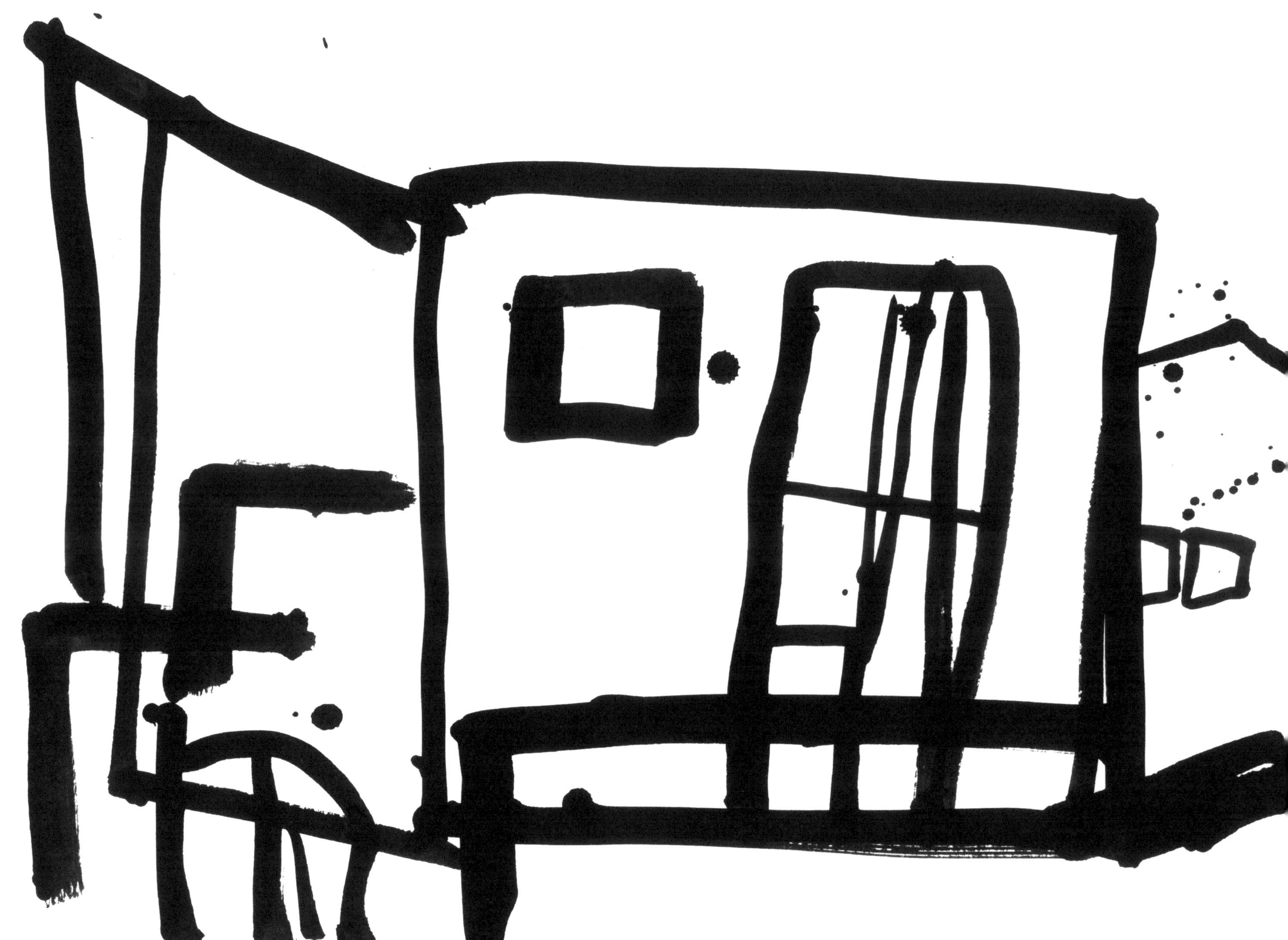

Sag Harbor

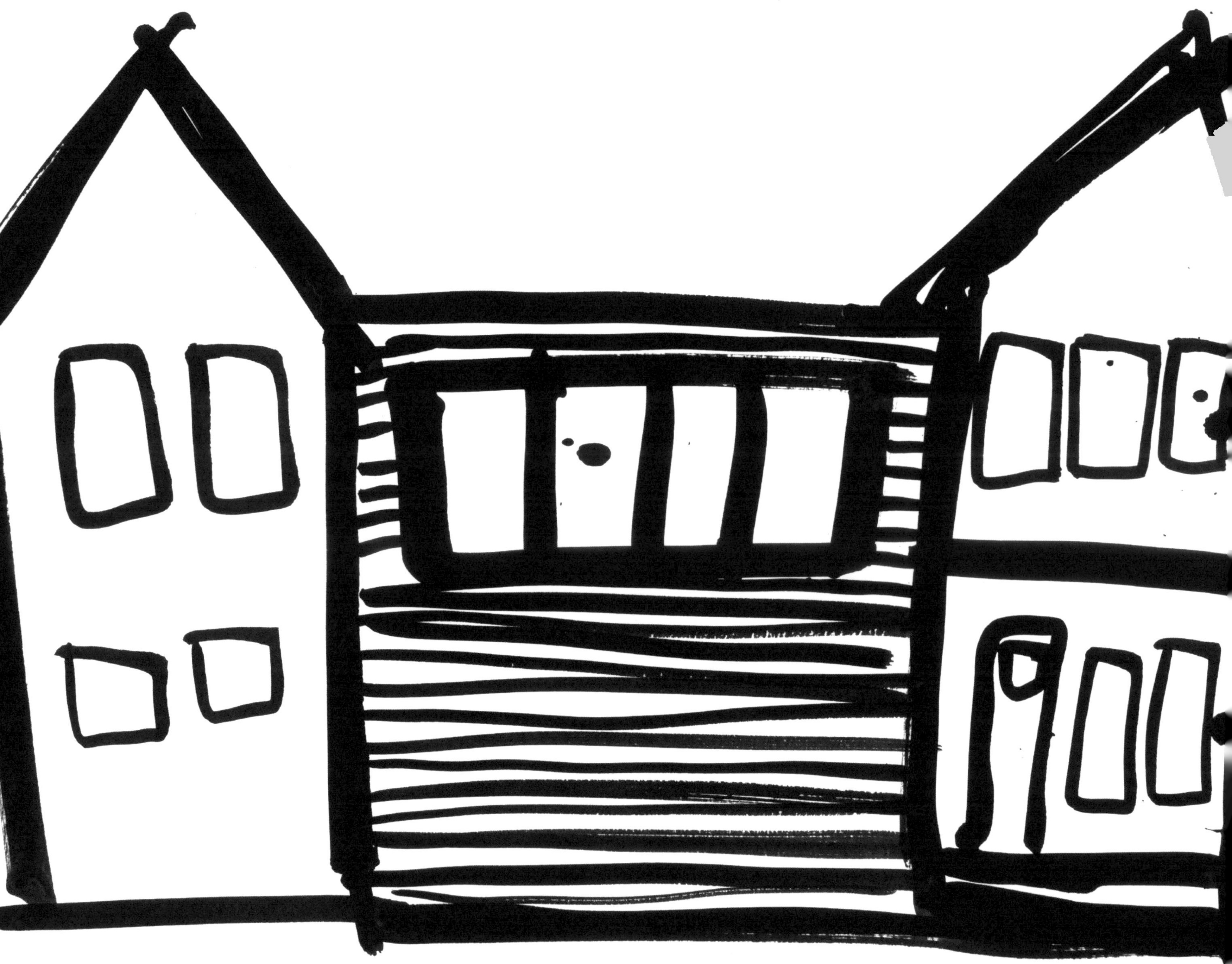

Dunes

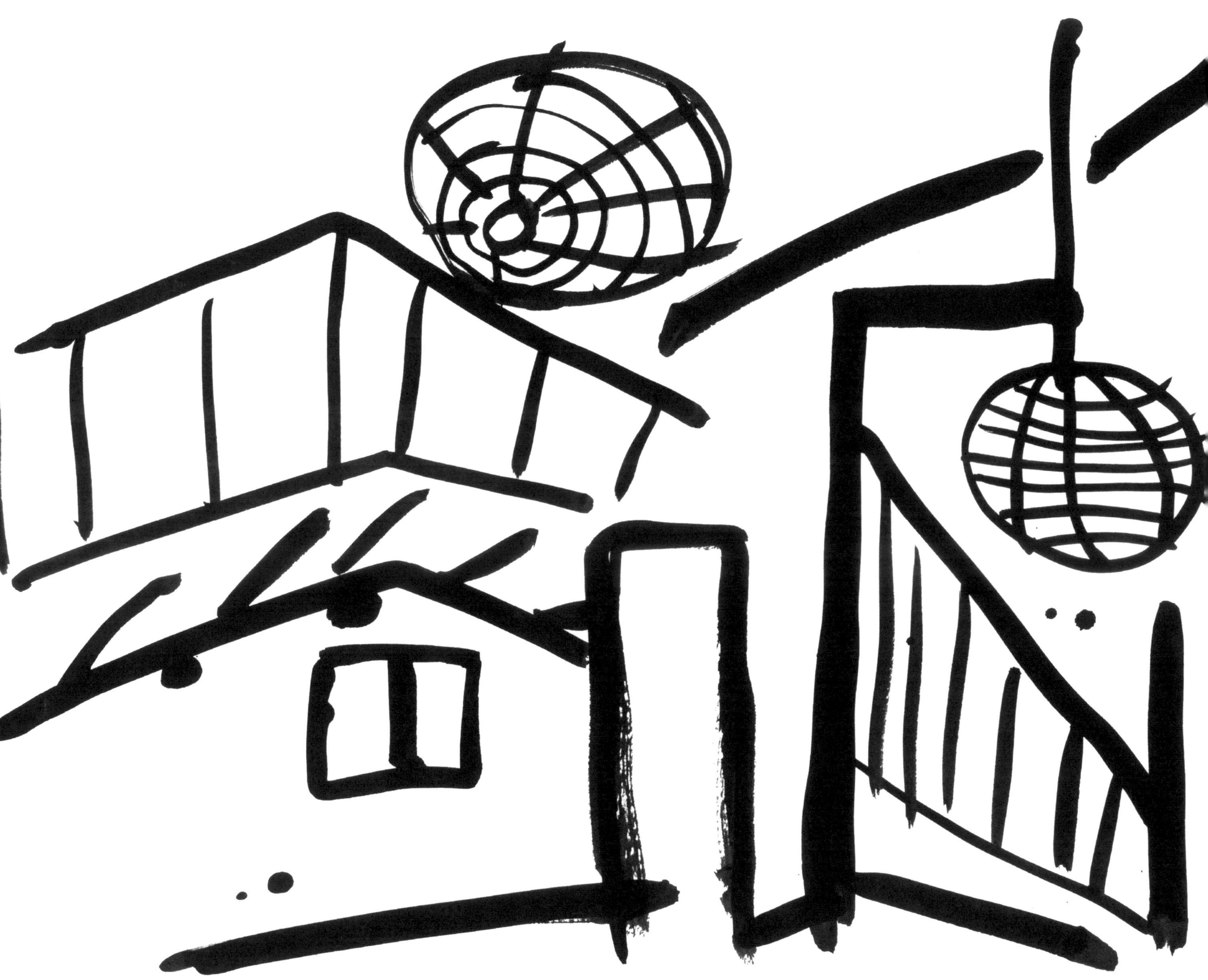

Dunes

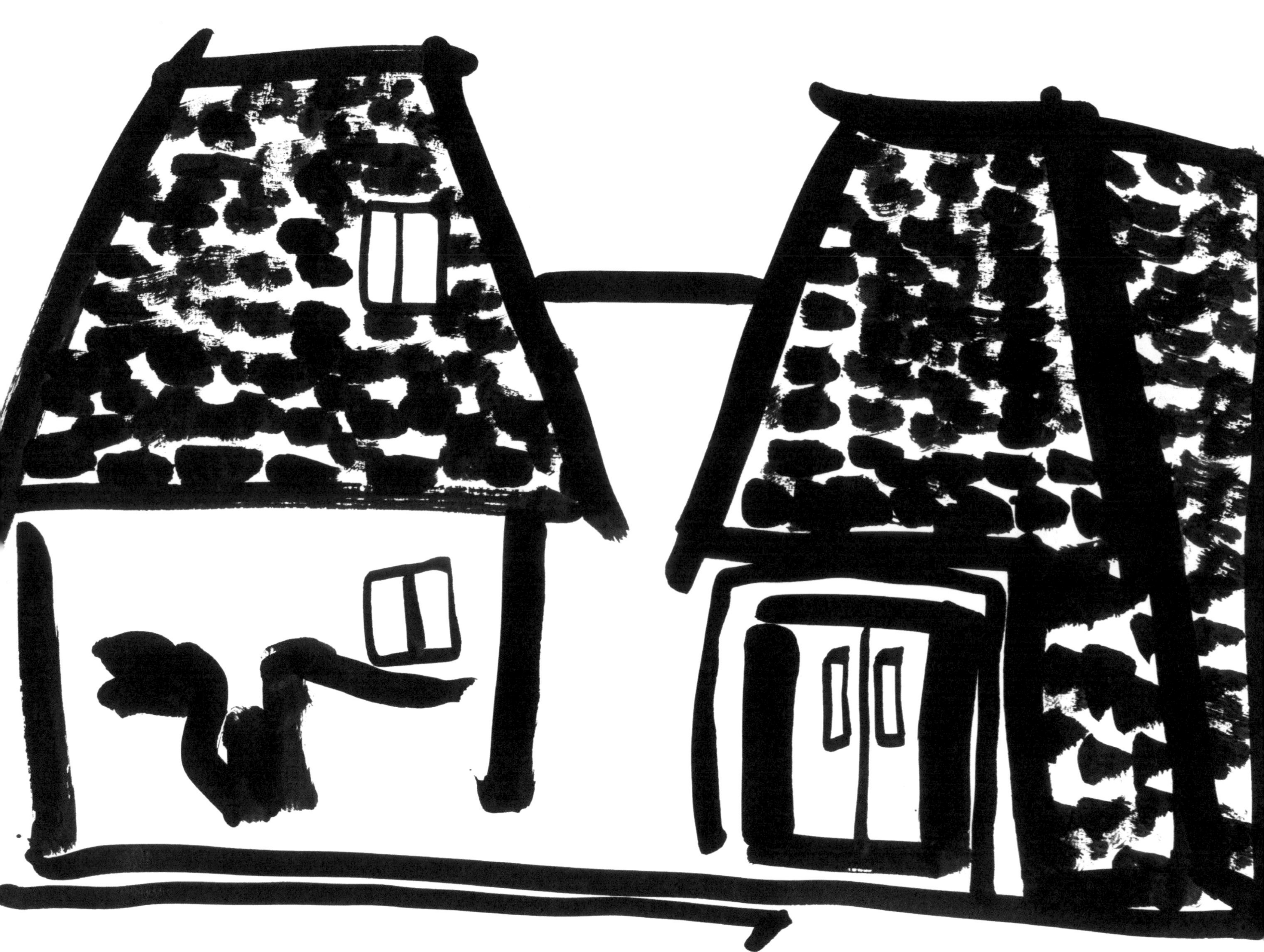

Lynn House, Andrew Geller, Westhampton Beach

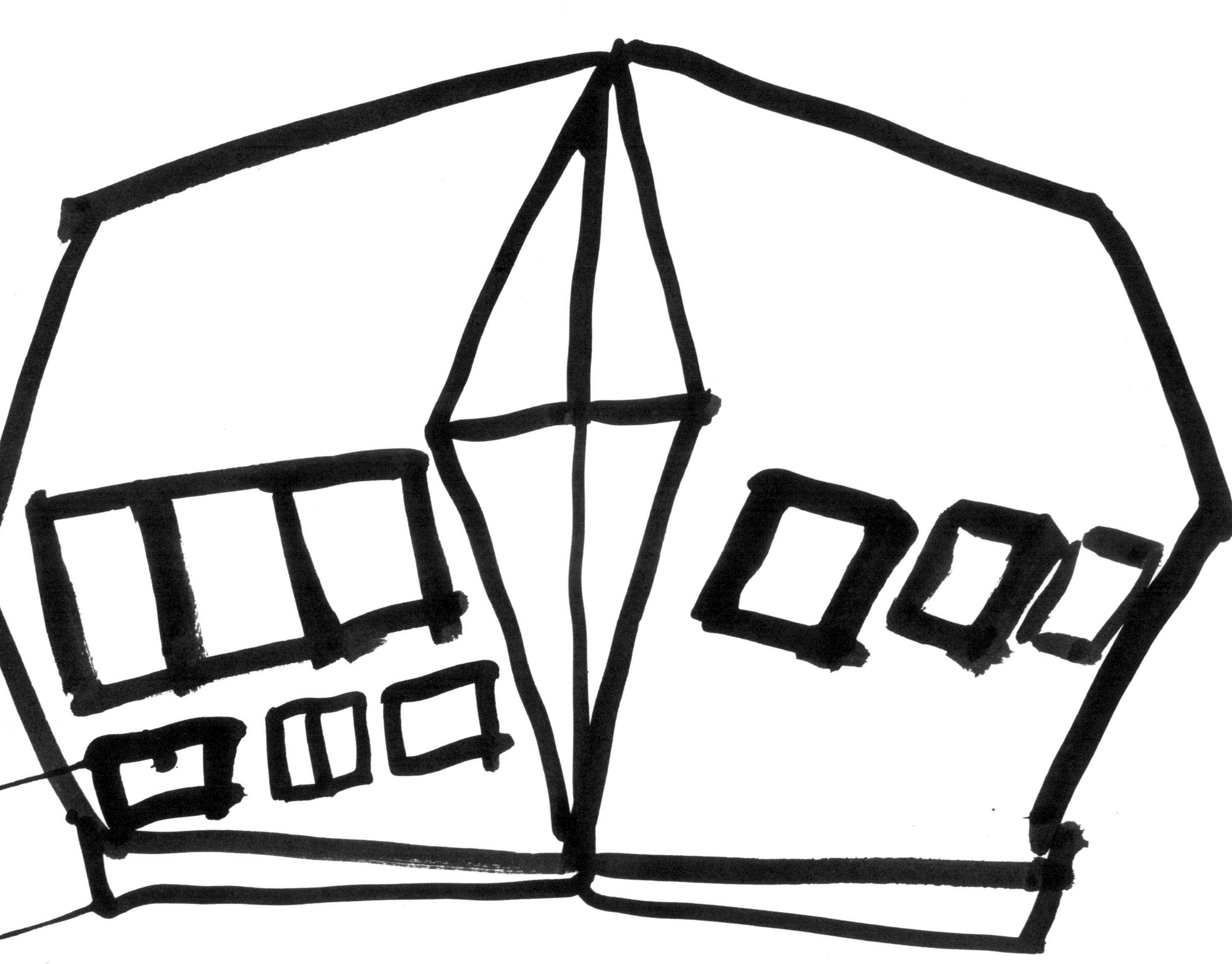

Frank House, Andrew Geller, Fire Island

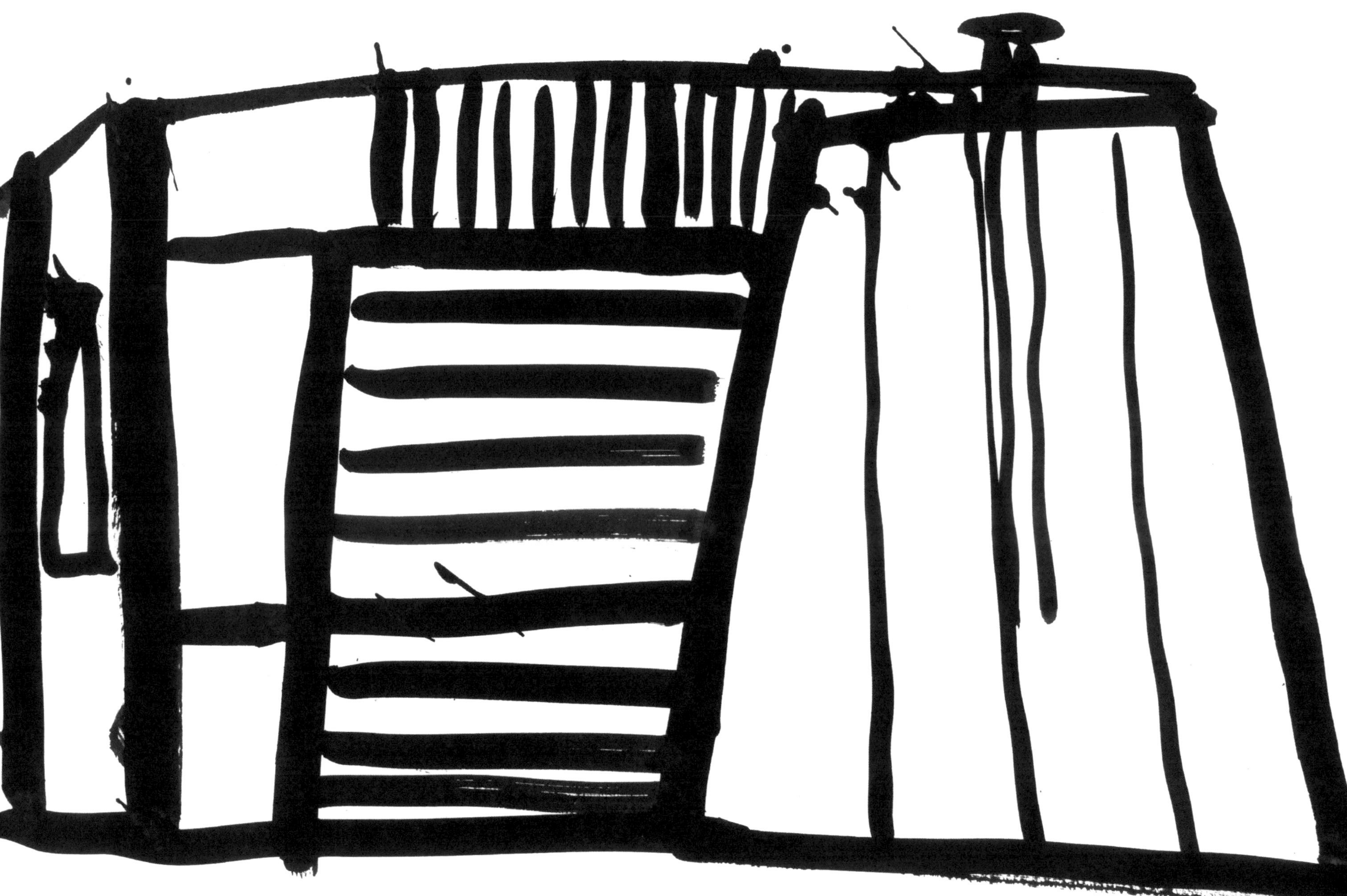

Amagansett

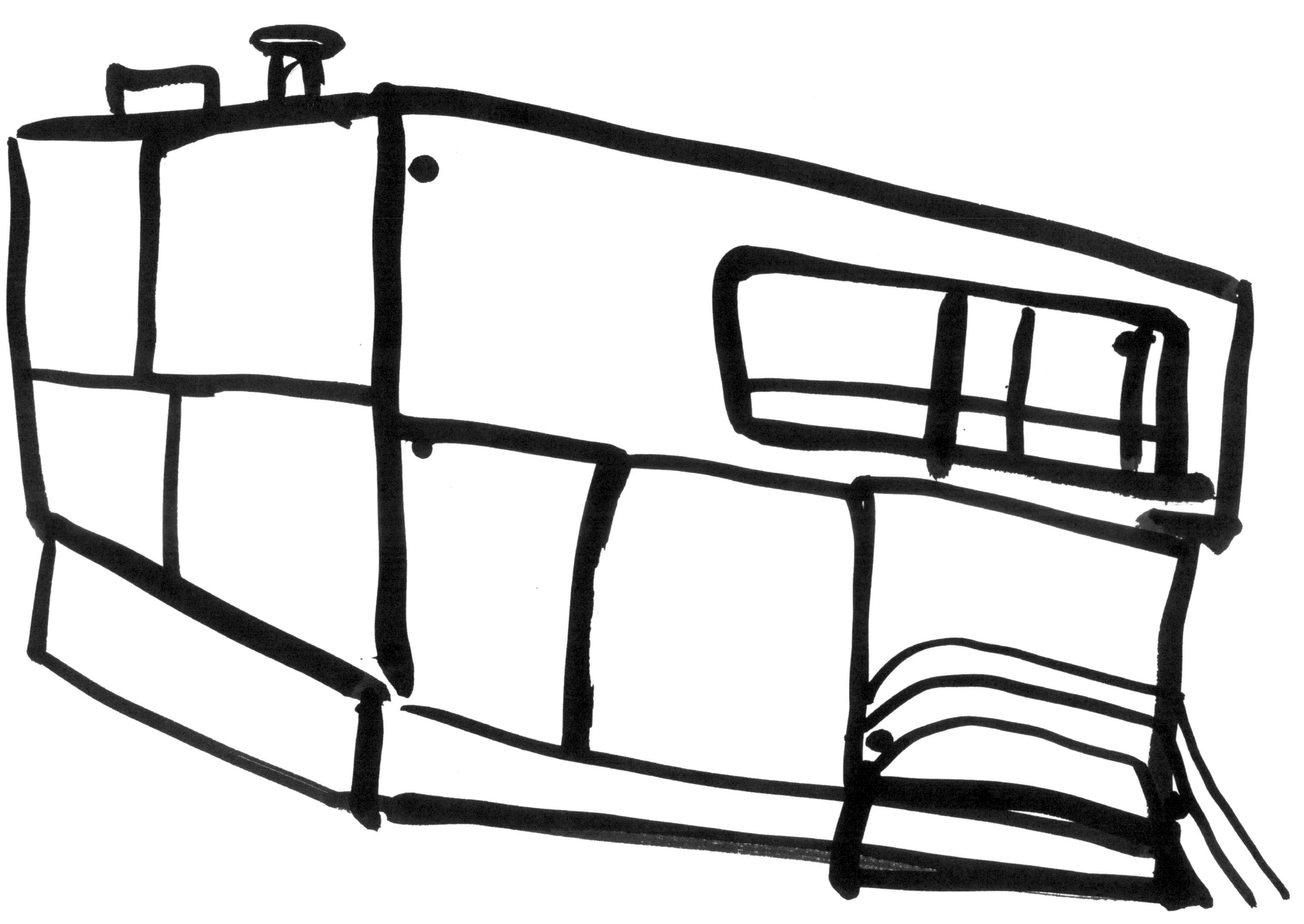

Dunes

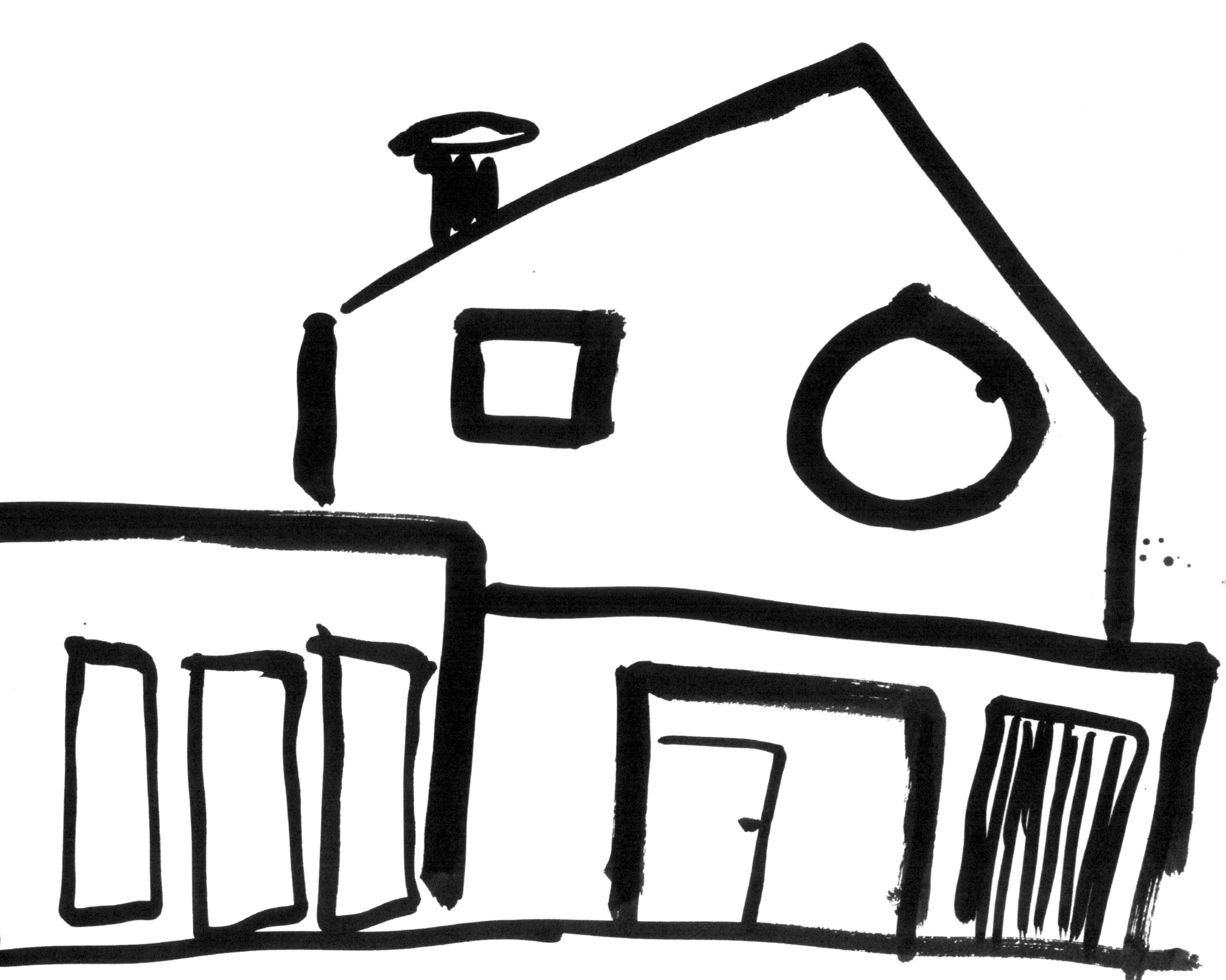

Andrew Geller, Sag Harbor

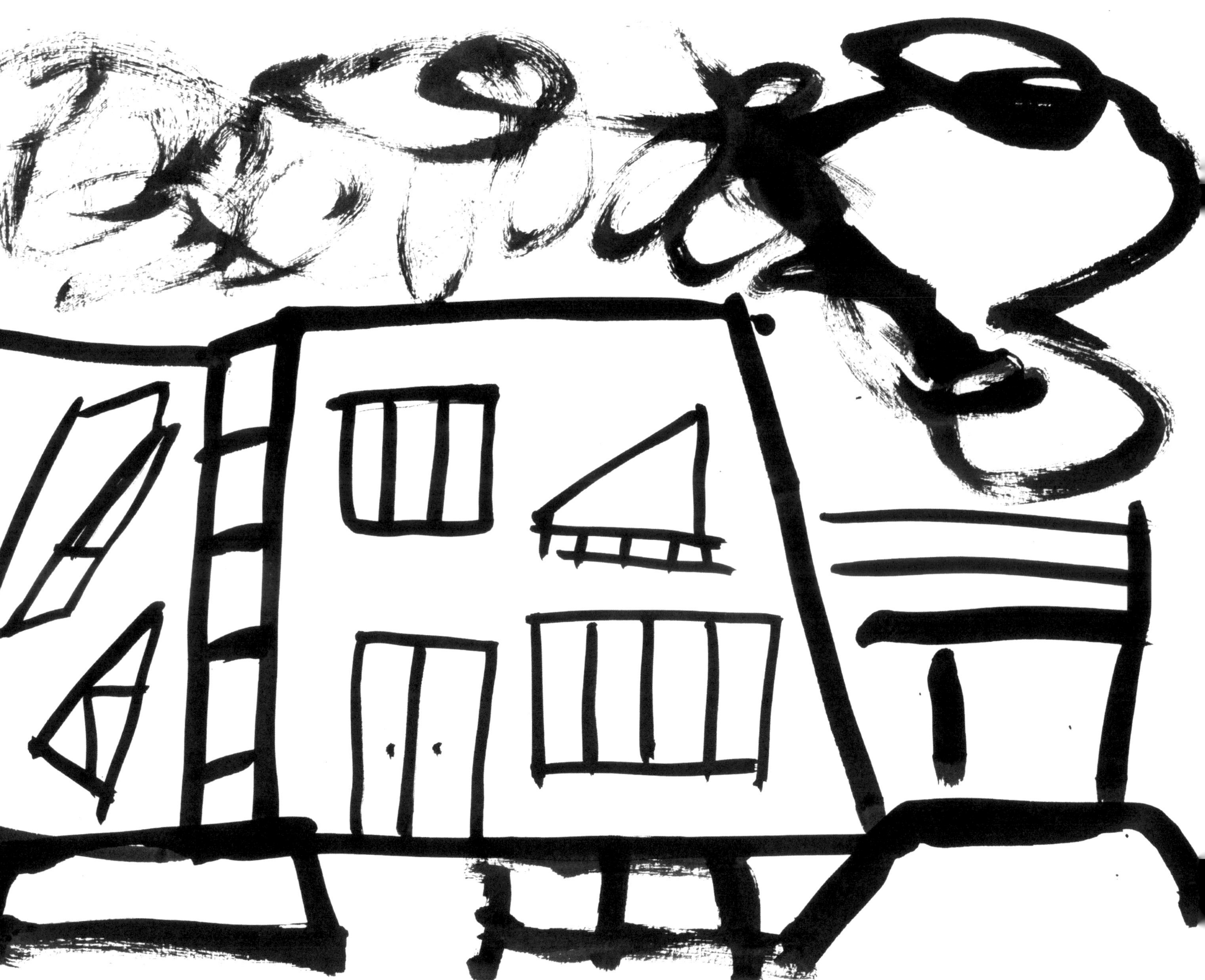

Andrew Geller, Sag Harbor

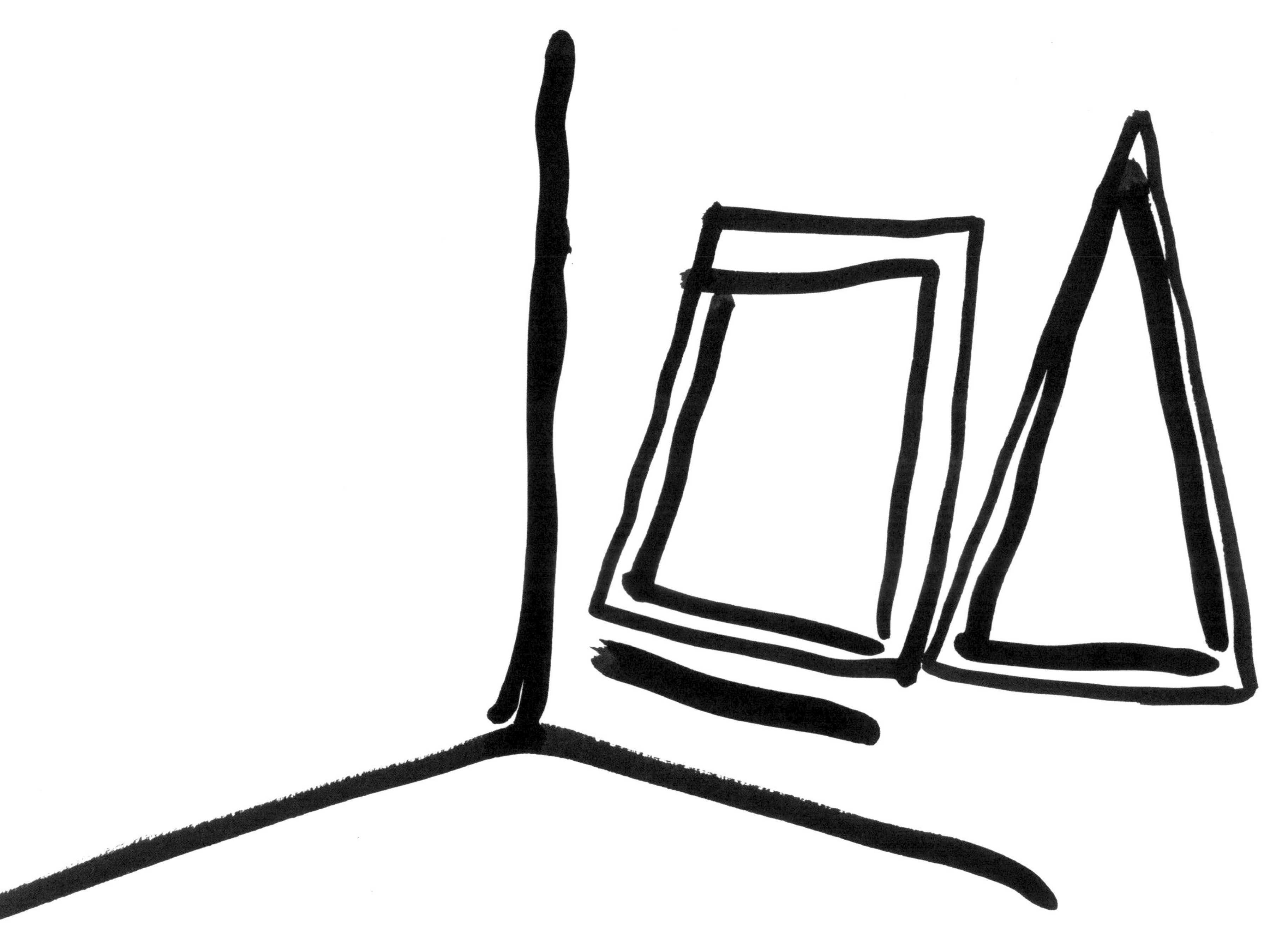

Andrew Geller, Sag Harbor

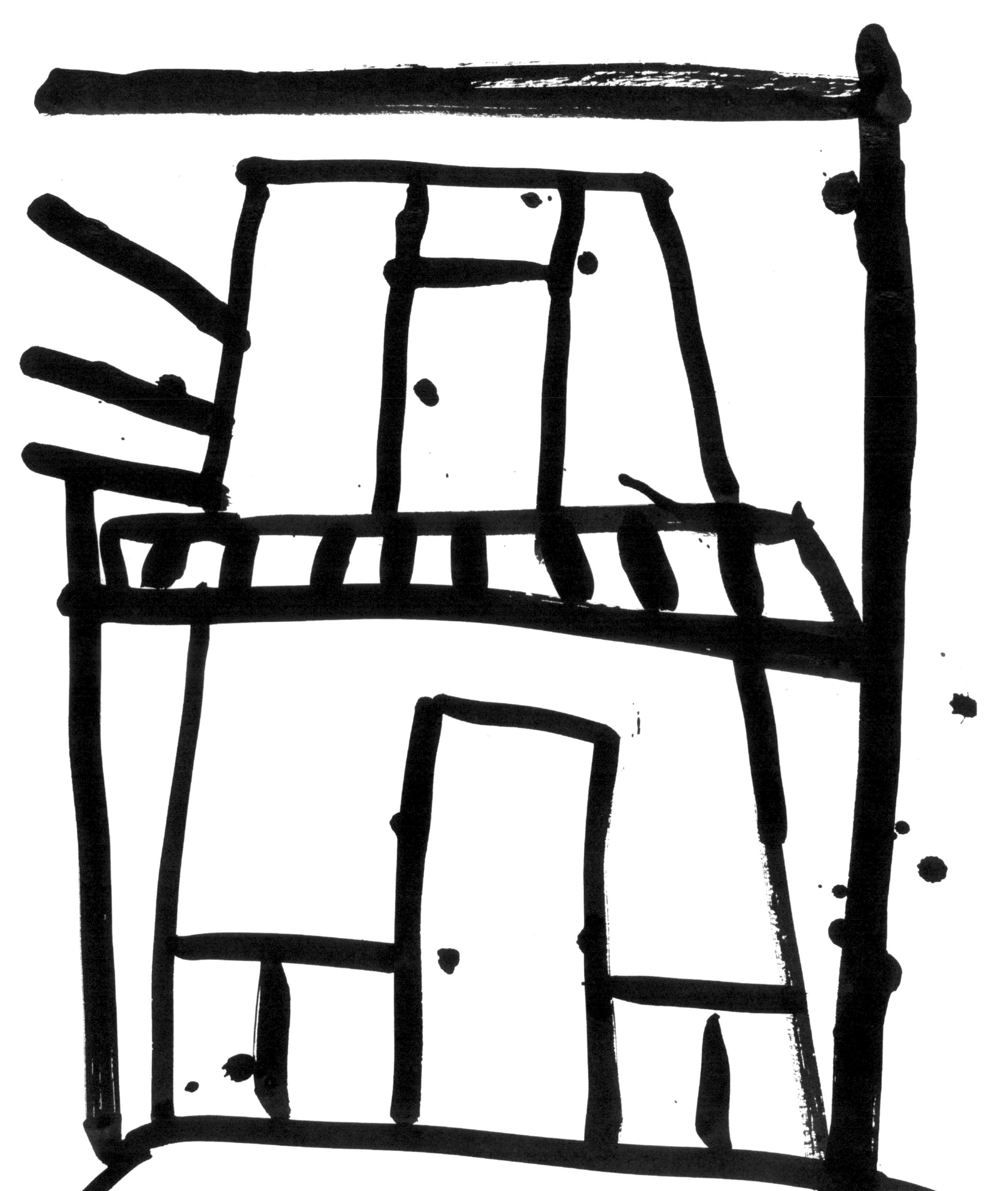

Andrew Geller, Sag Harbor

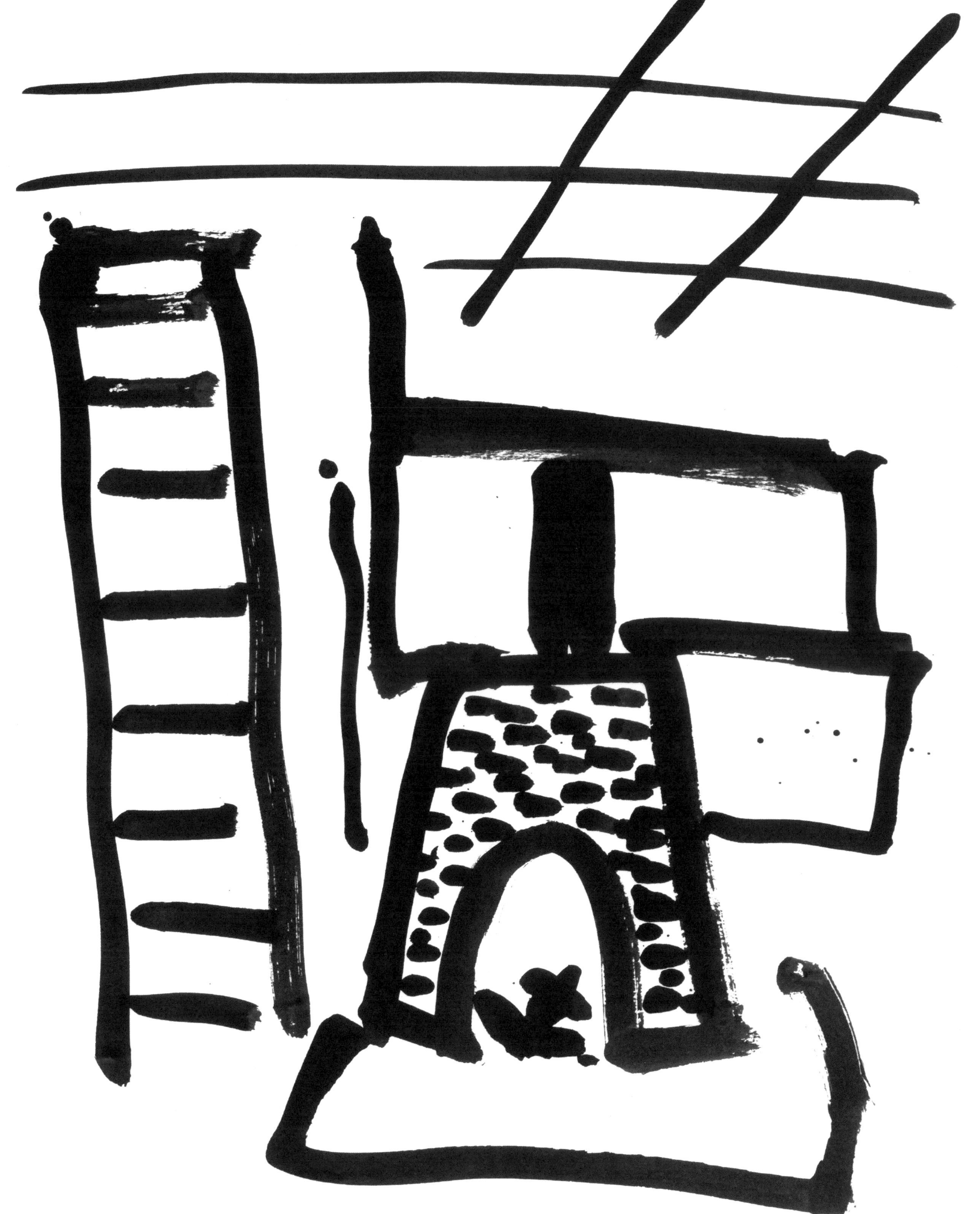

Andrew Geller, Martha's Vineyard

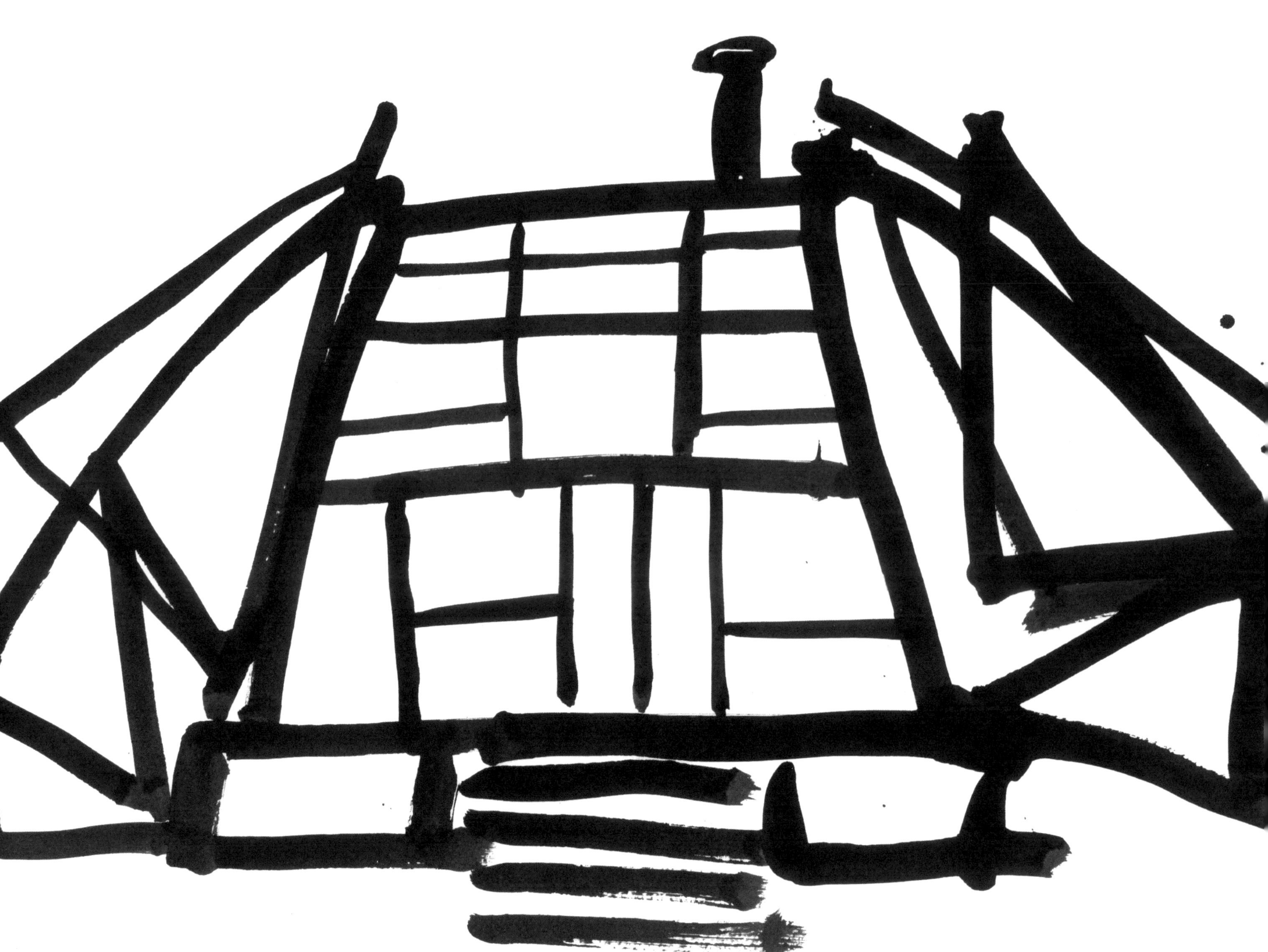

Andrew Geller, Sagaponack

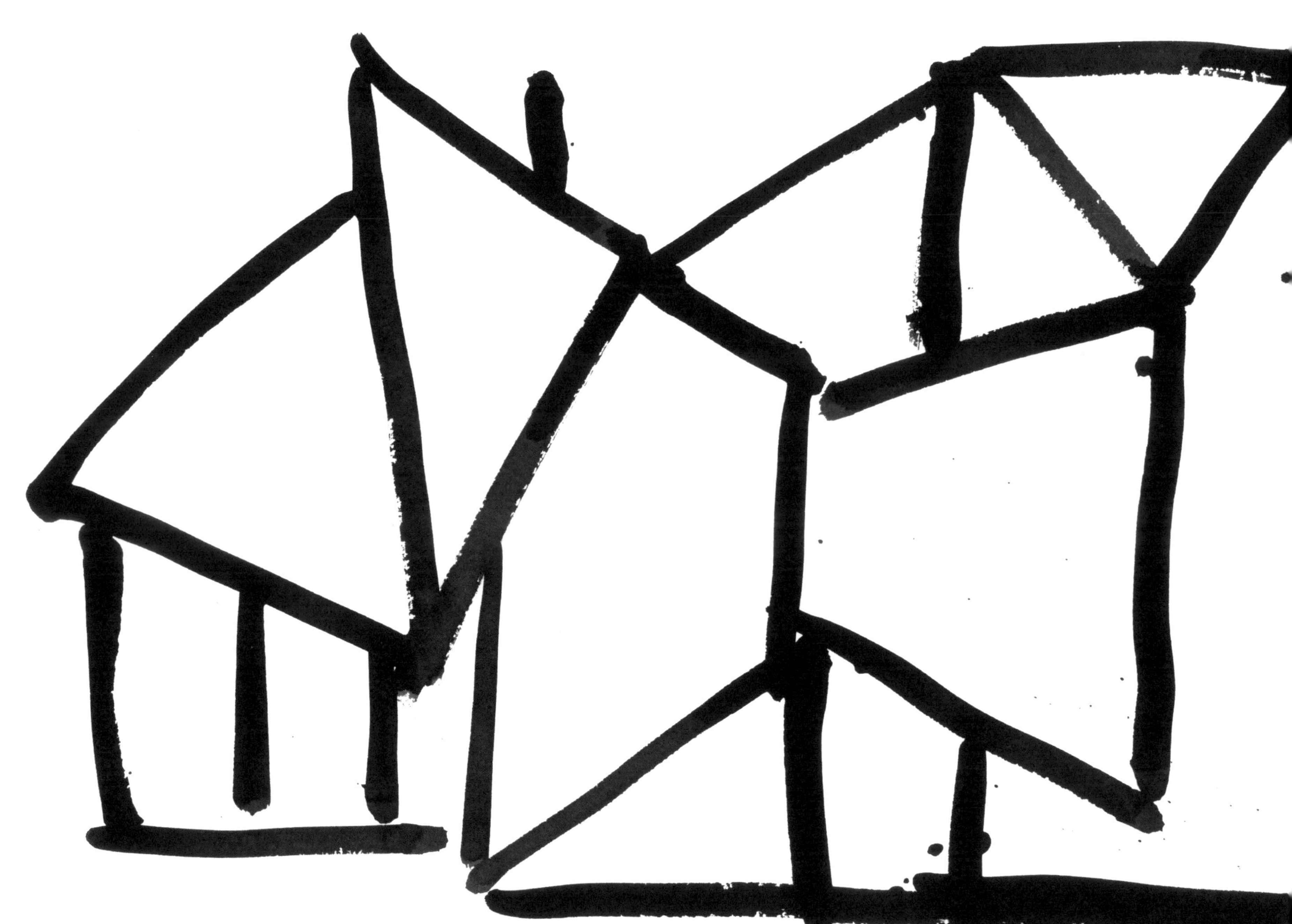

Andrew Geller, Sagaponack

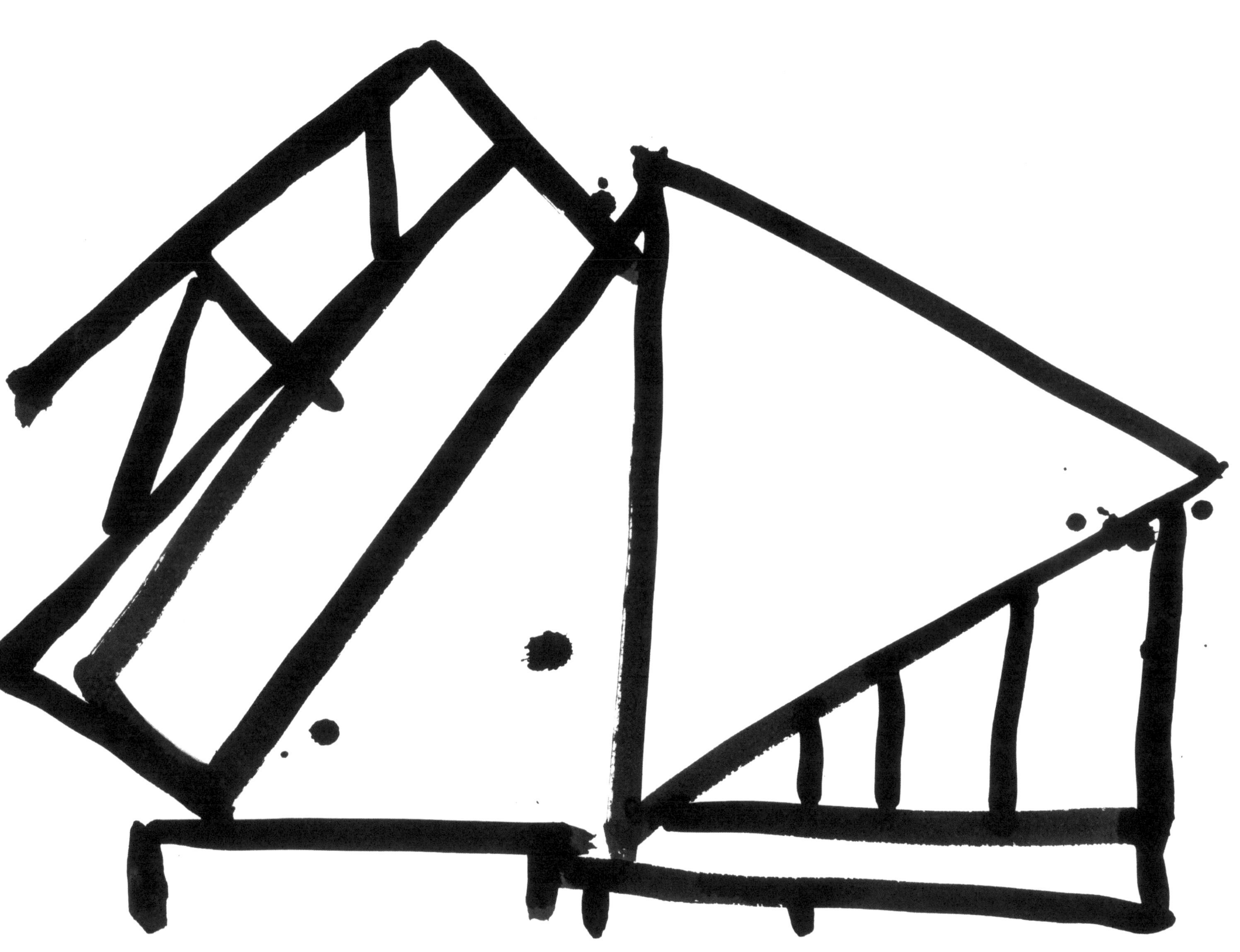

Northwest Harbor

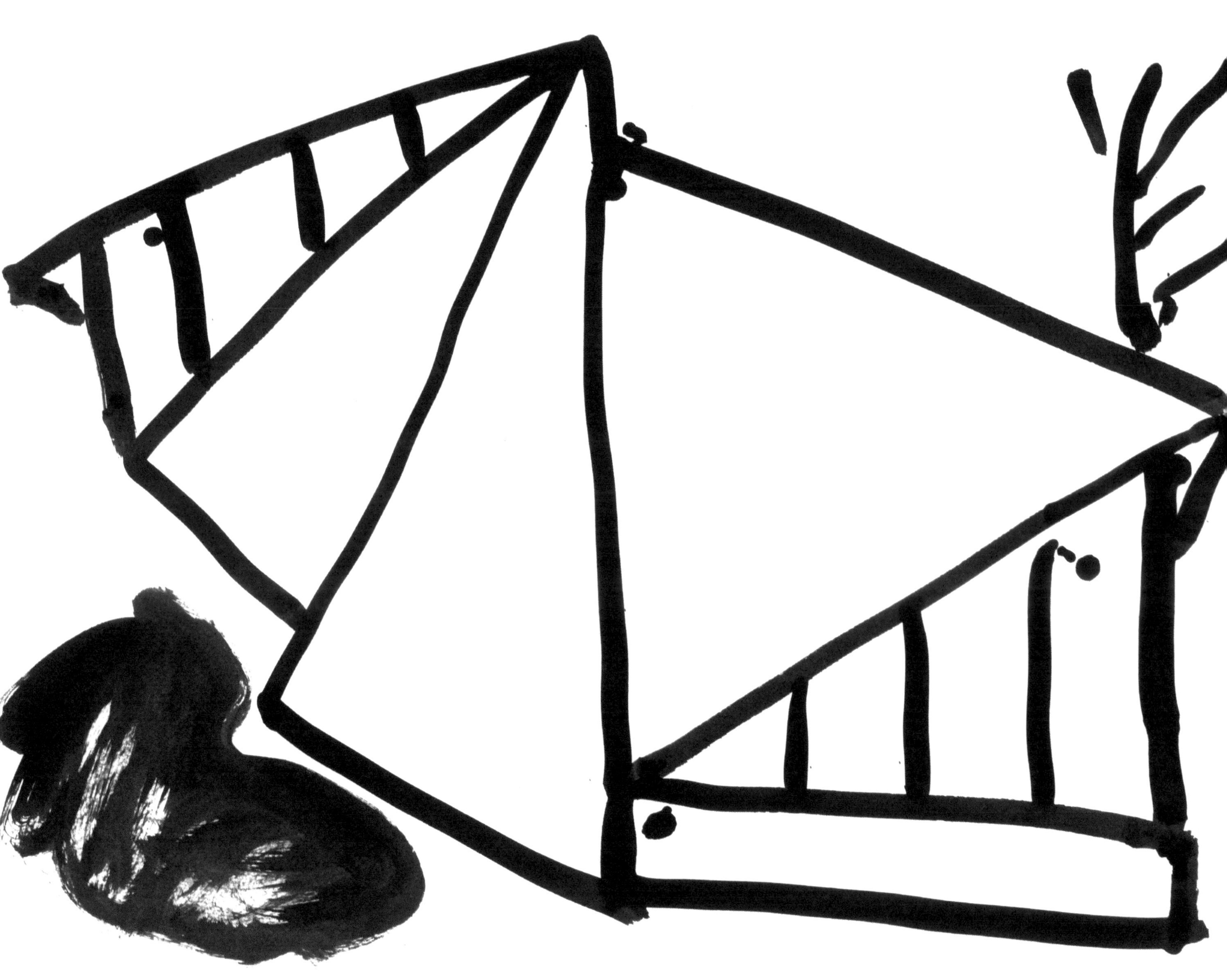

Andrew Geller, Martha's Vineyard

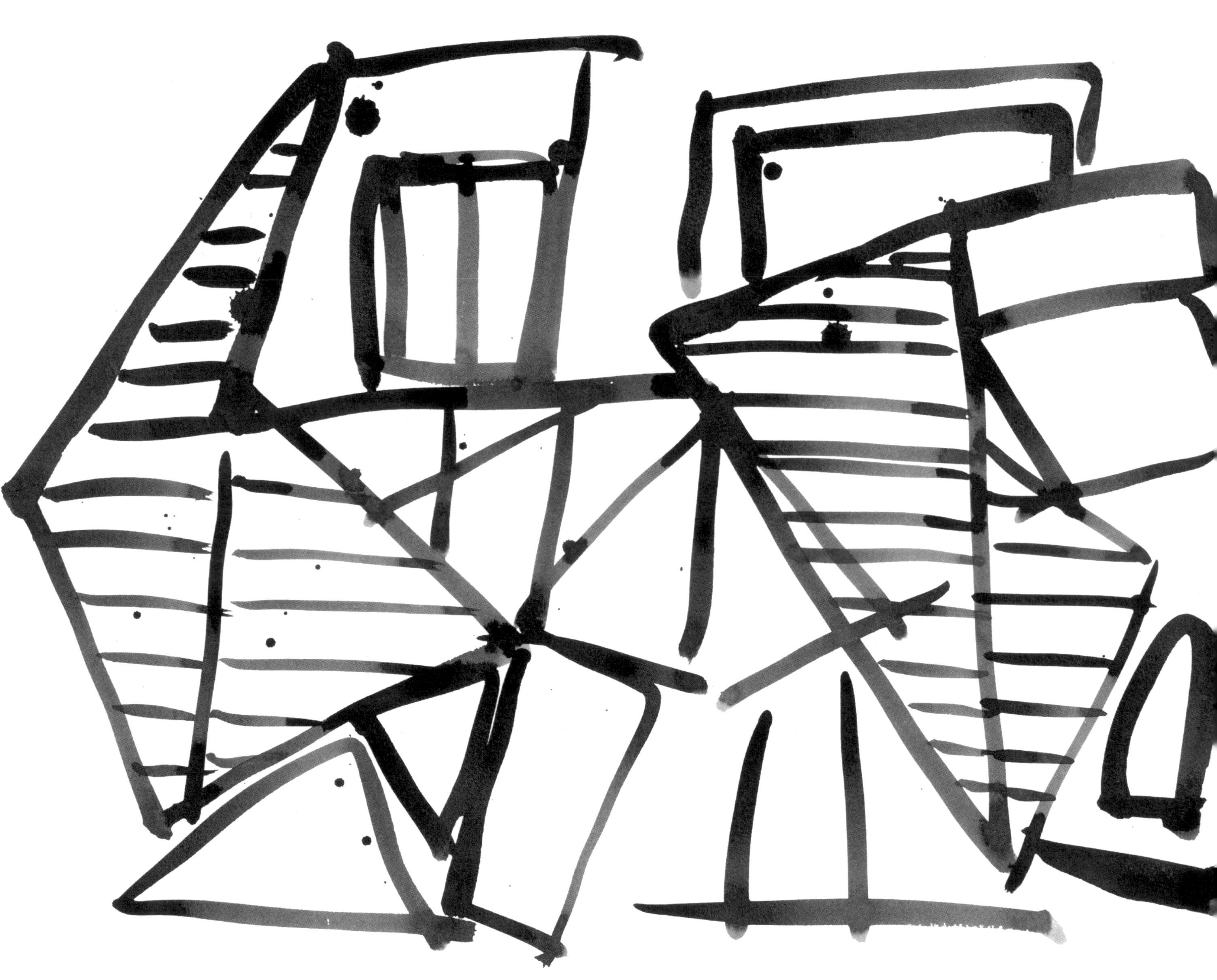

Northwest Harbor

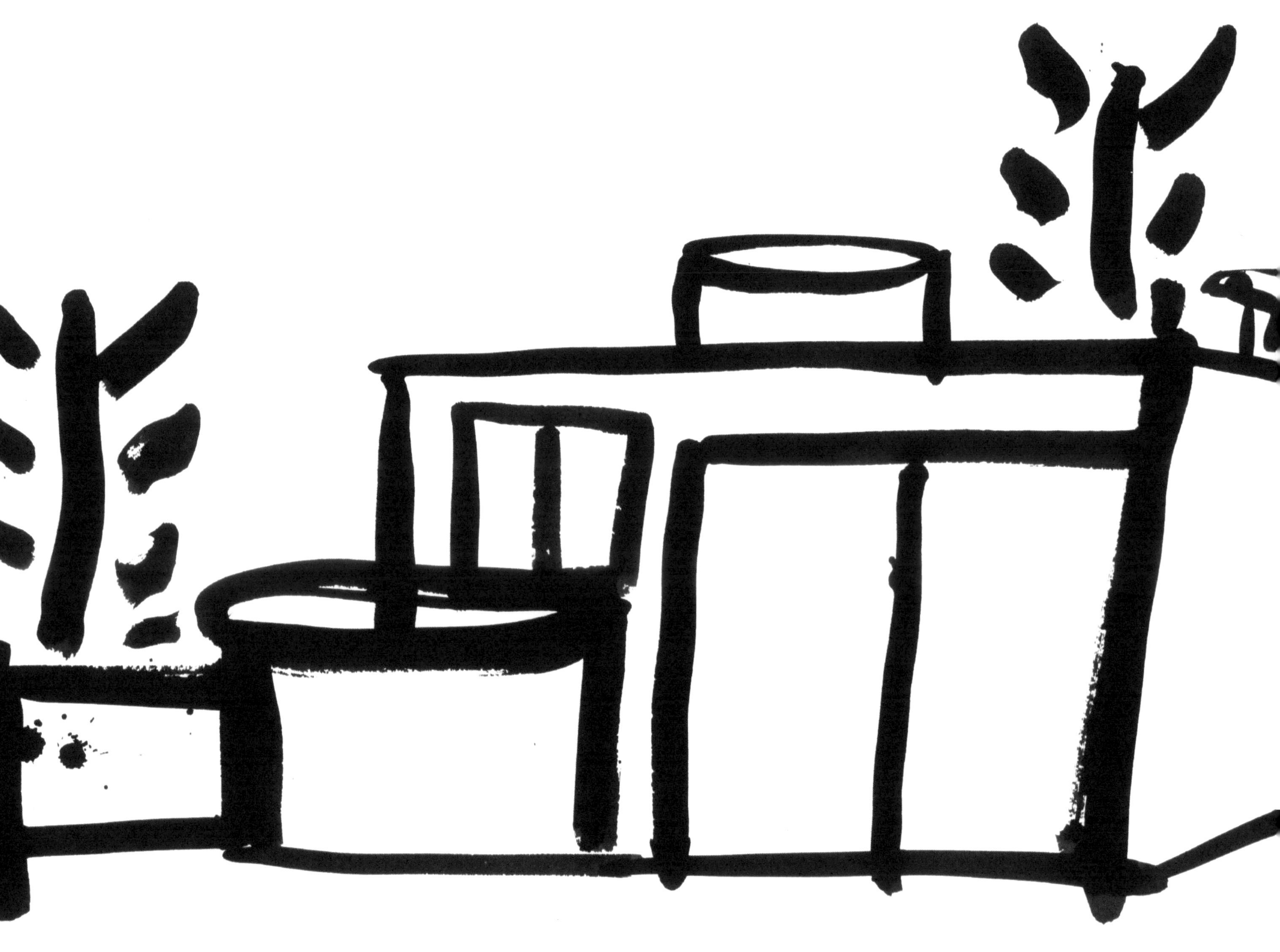

Elaine de Kooning House, Northwest Harbor

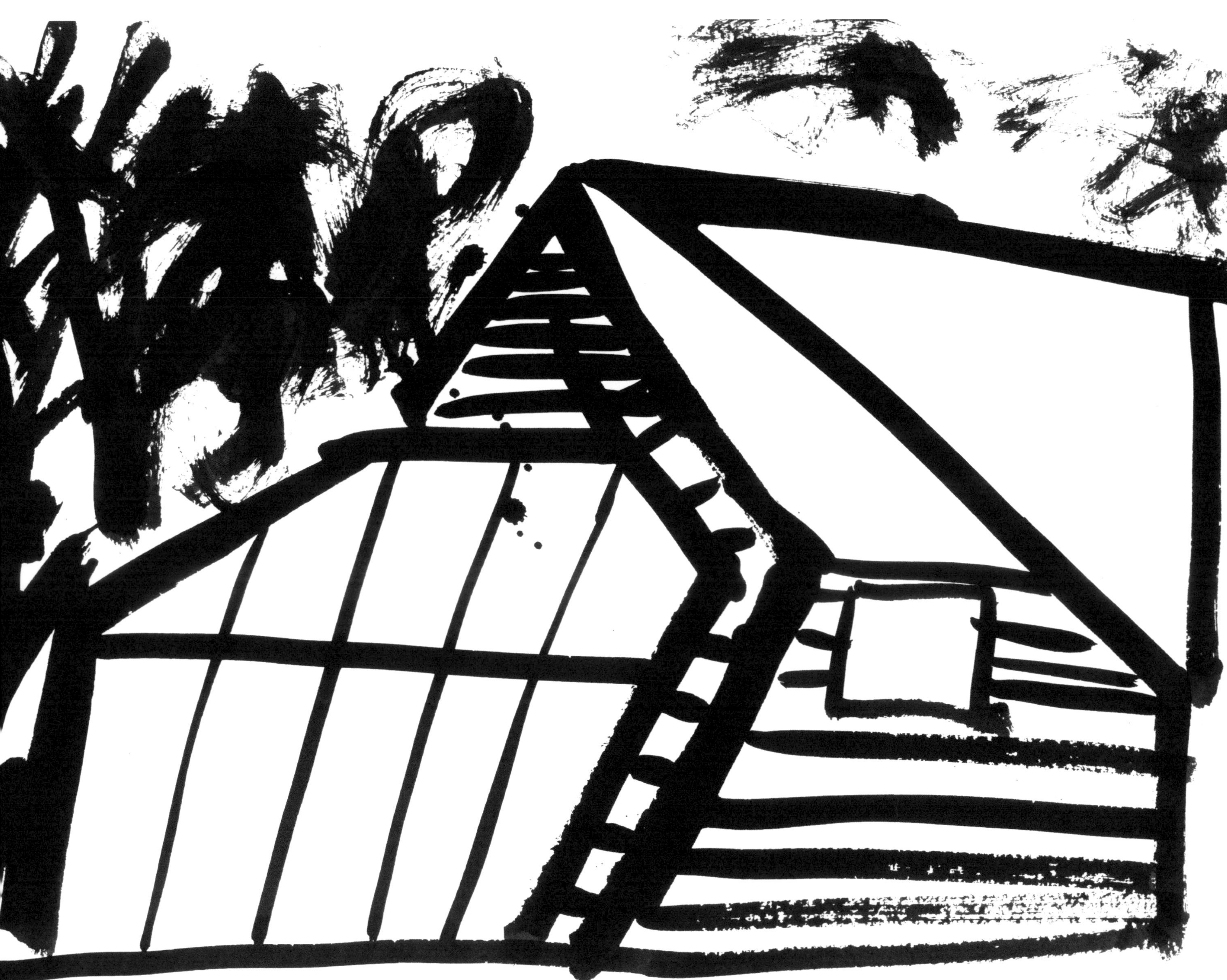

Dunes

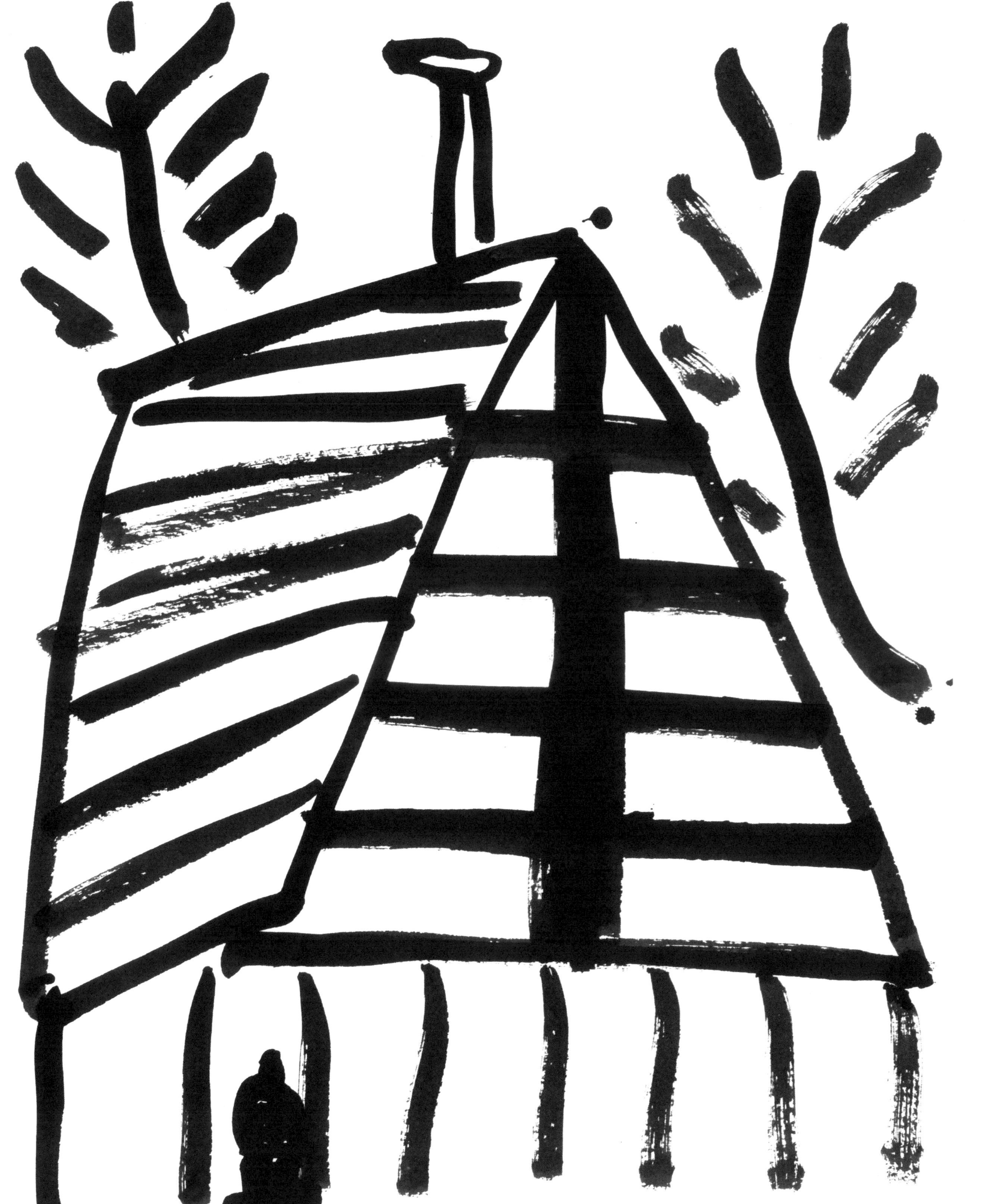

Dunes

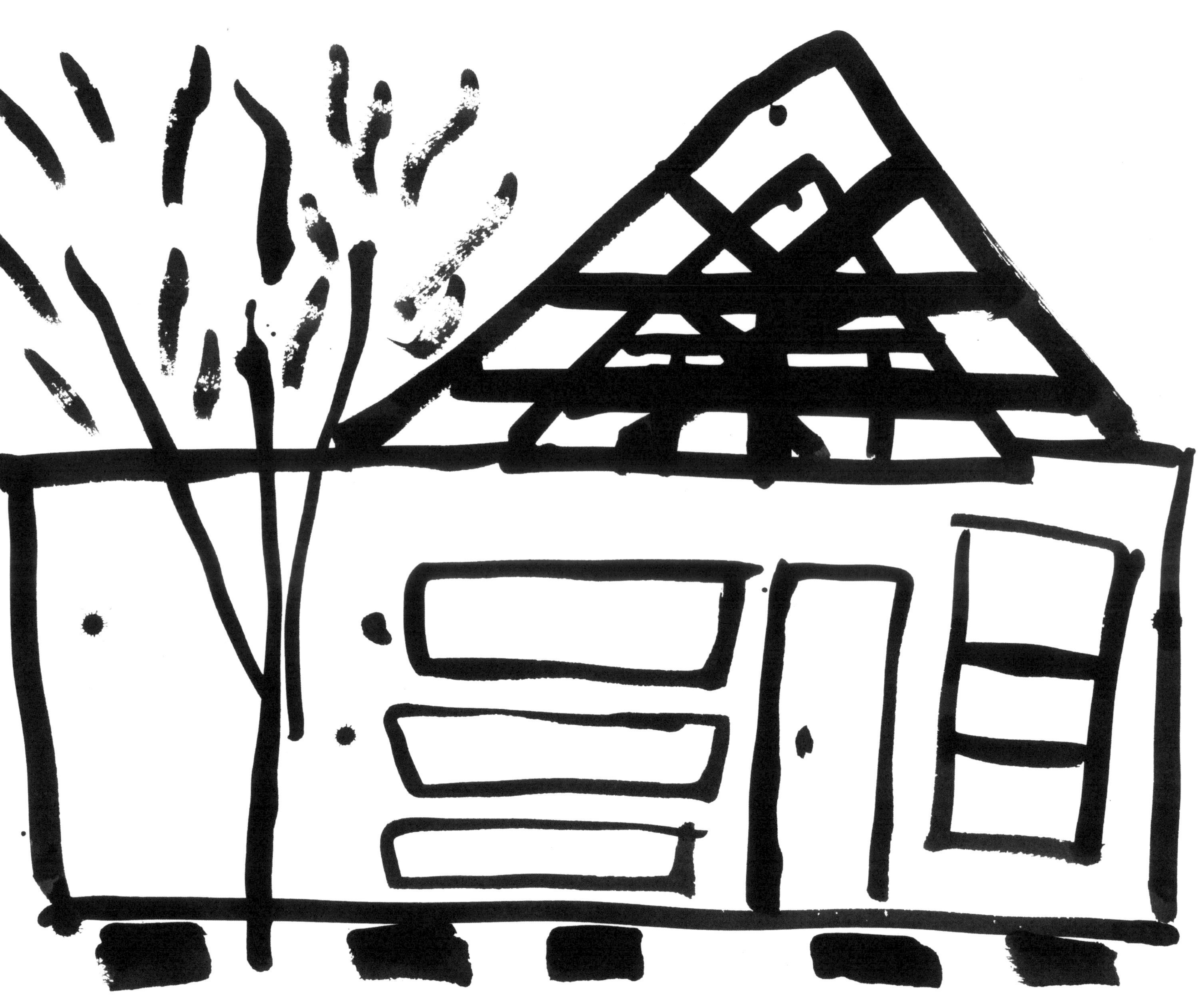

Dunes

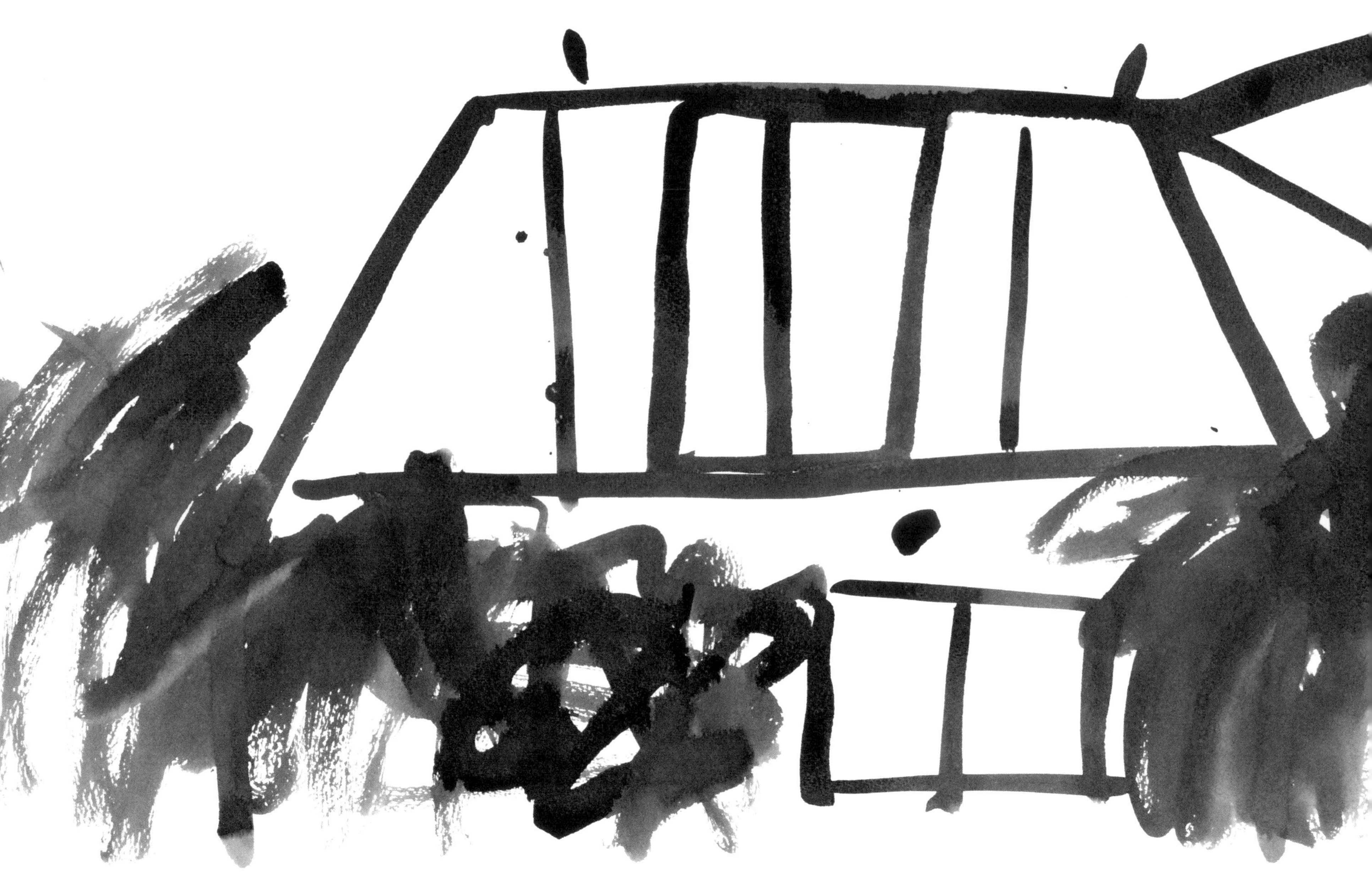

Dunes

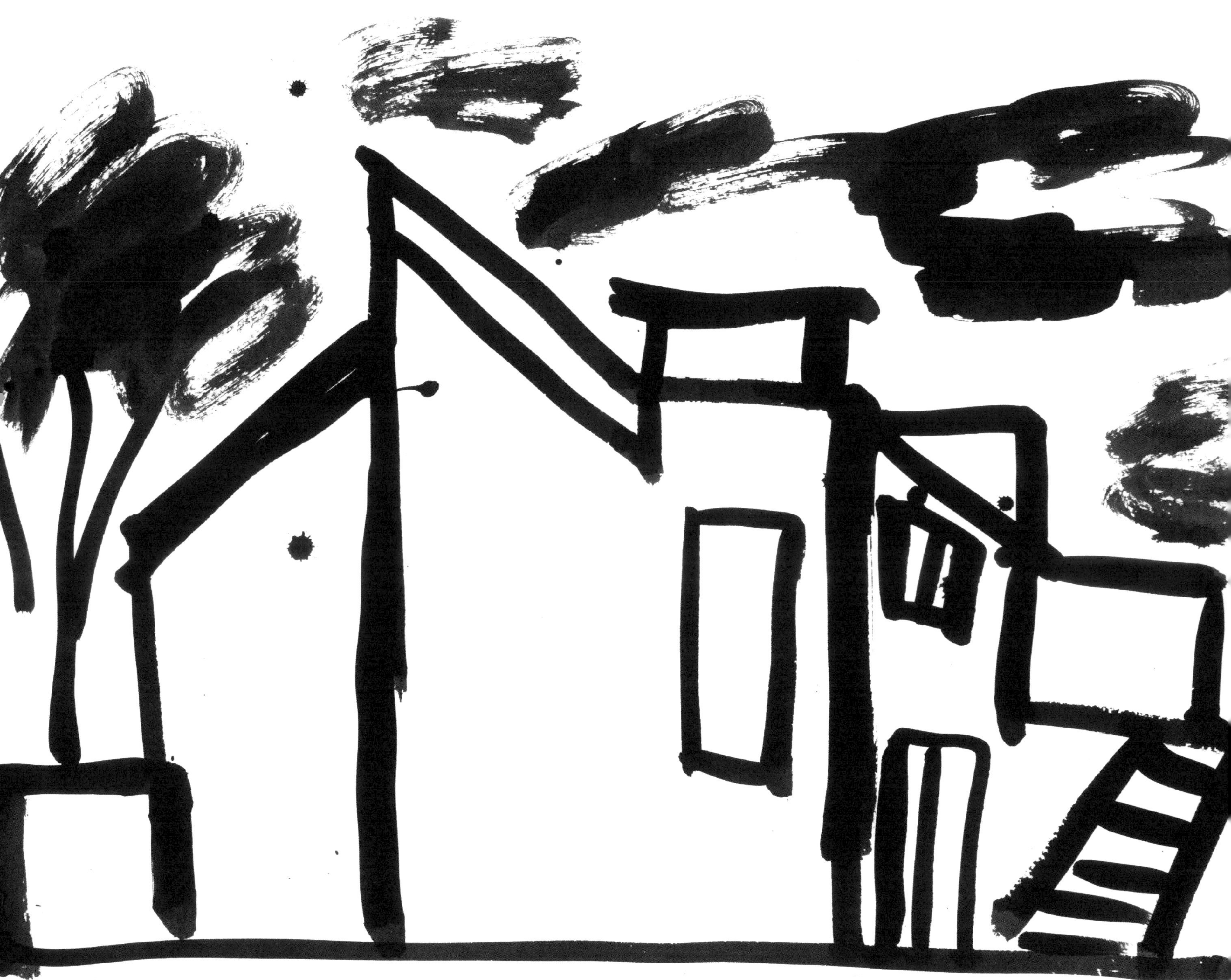

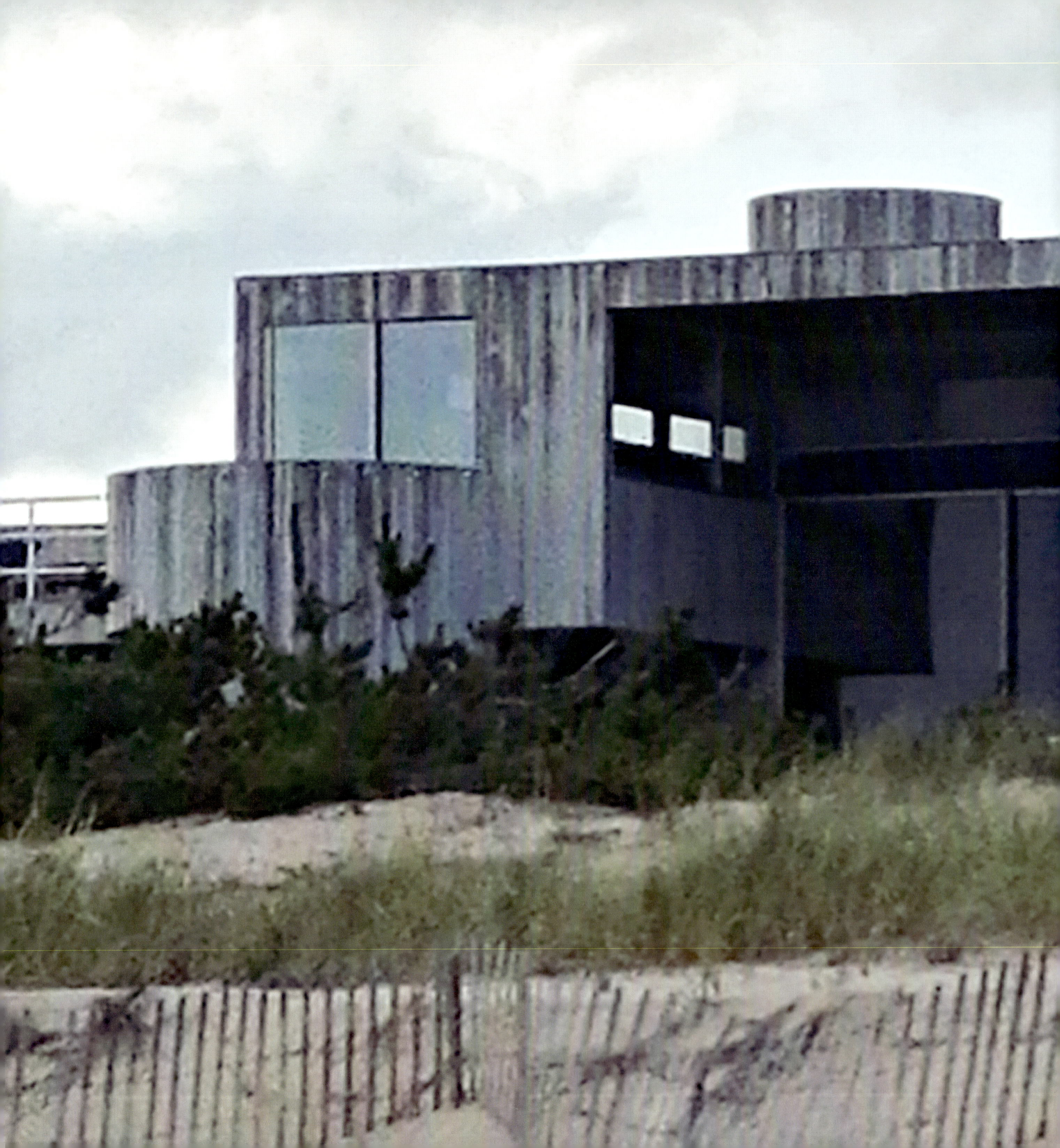

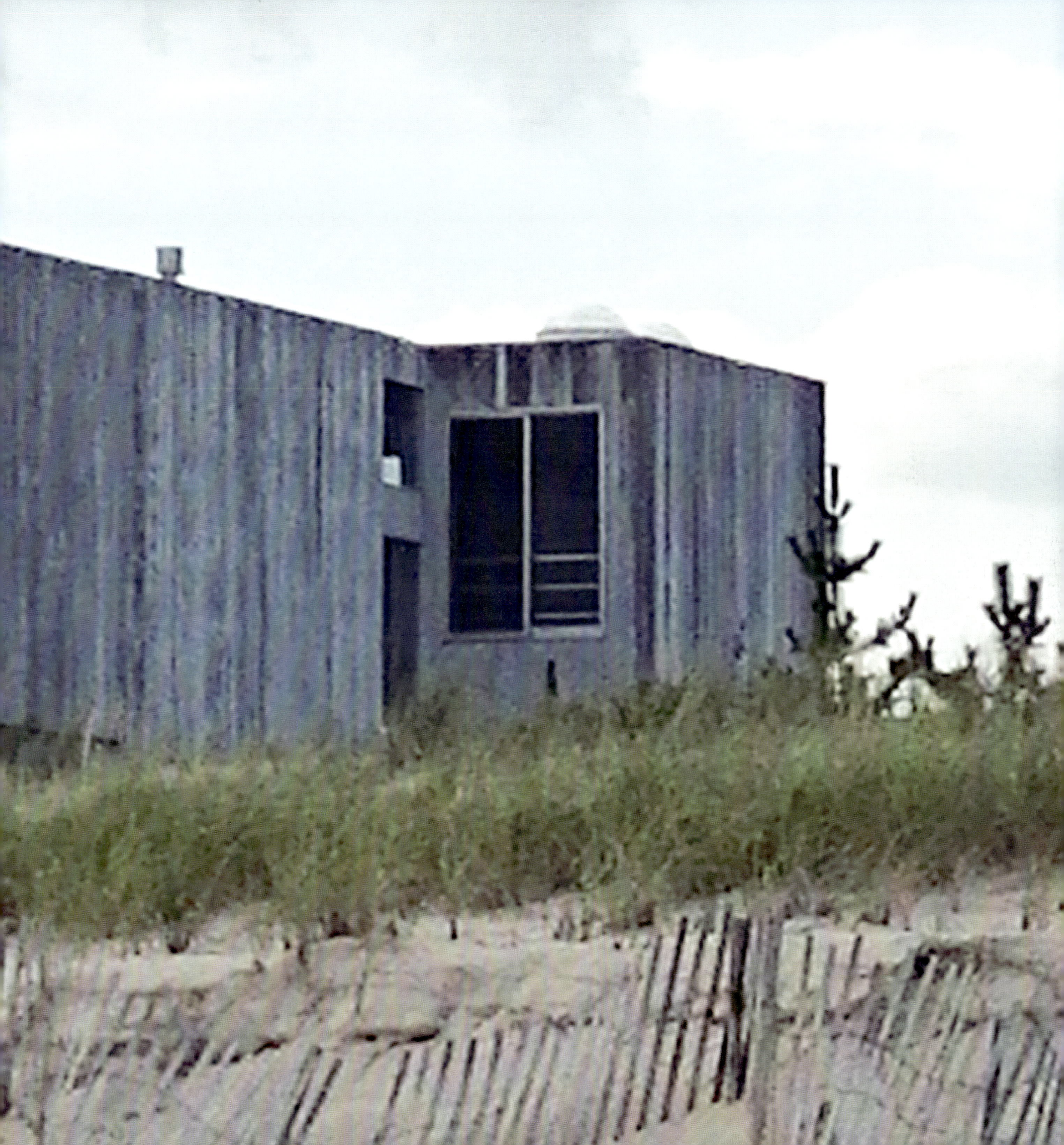

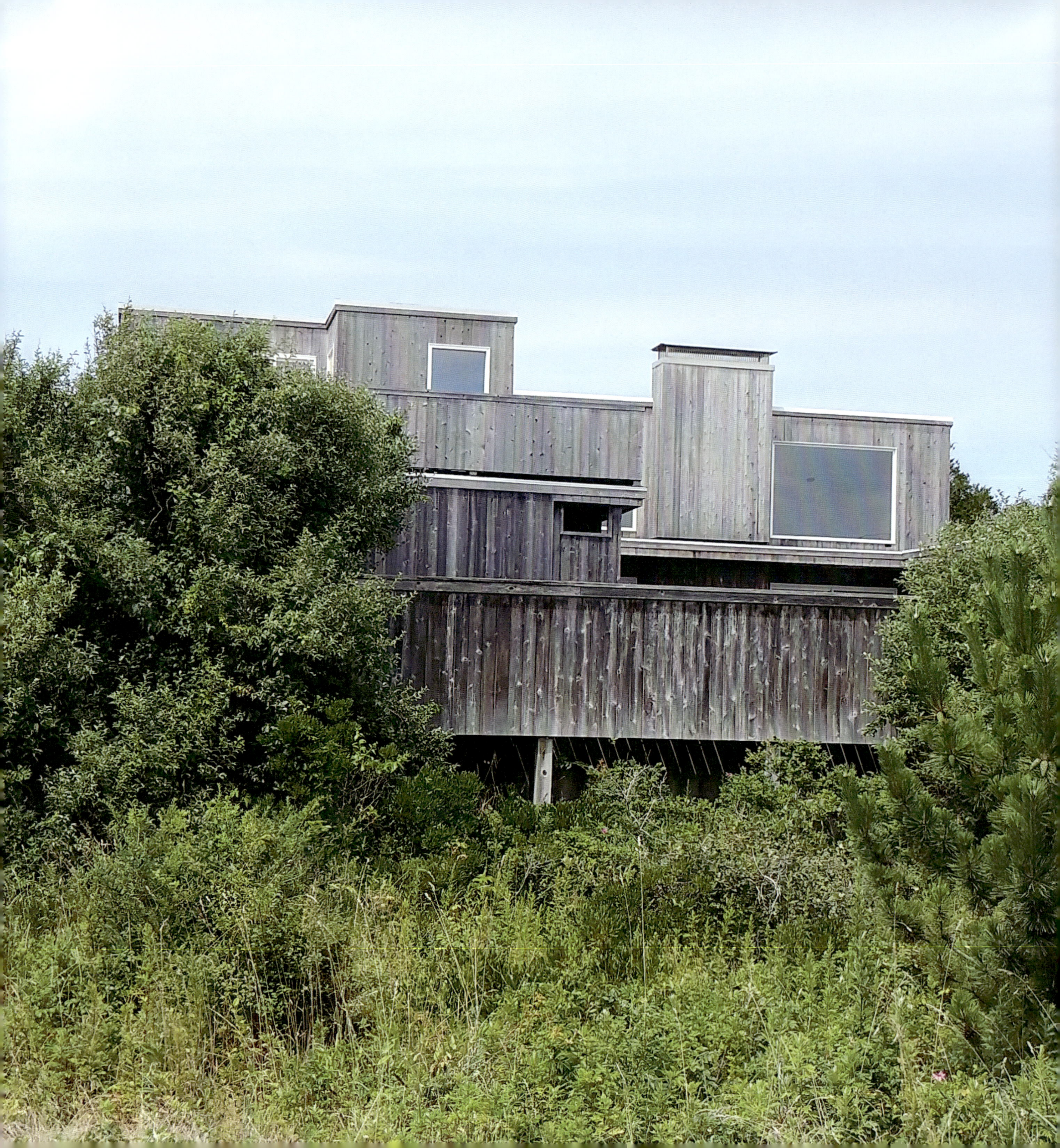

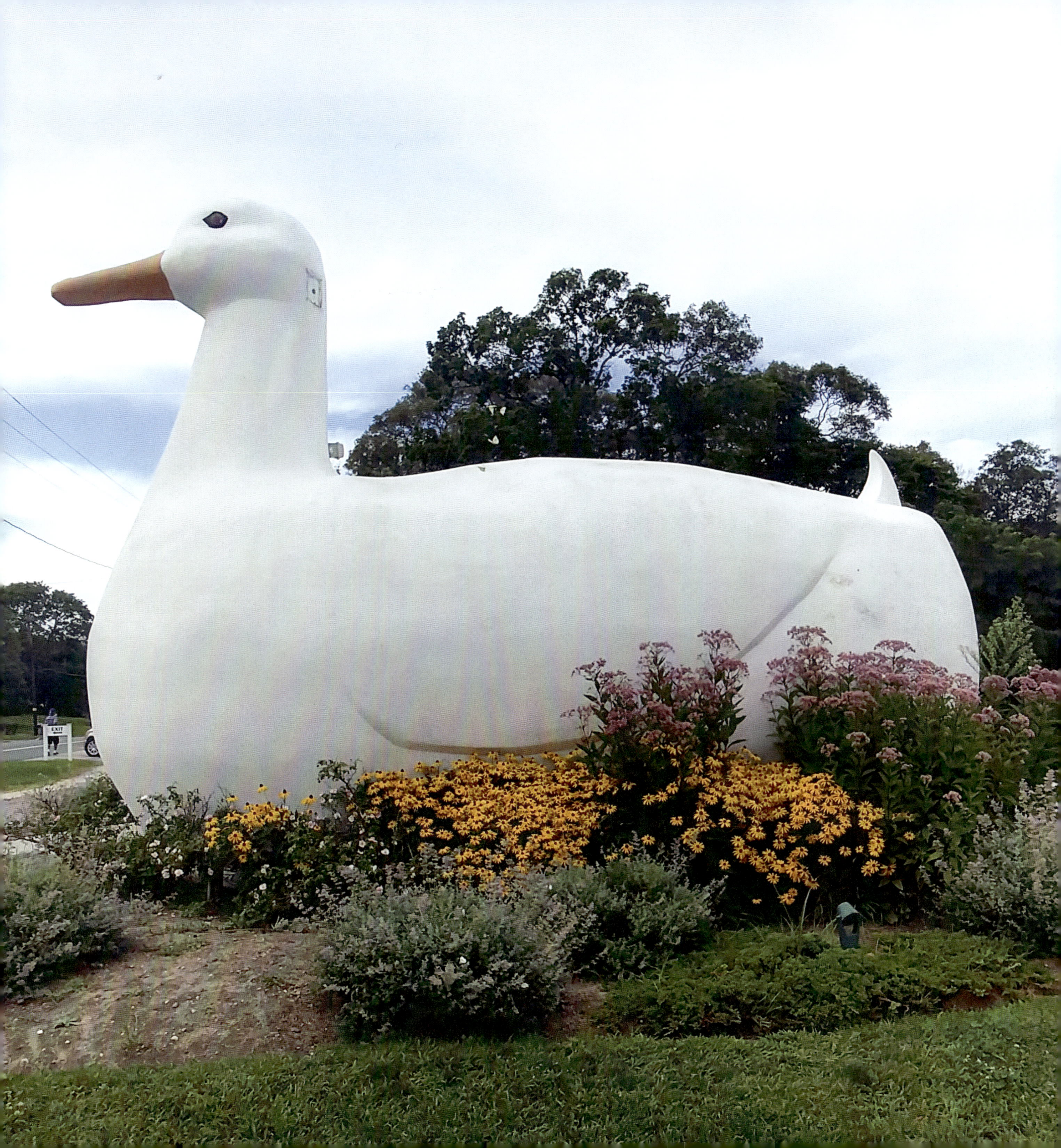

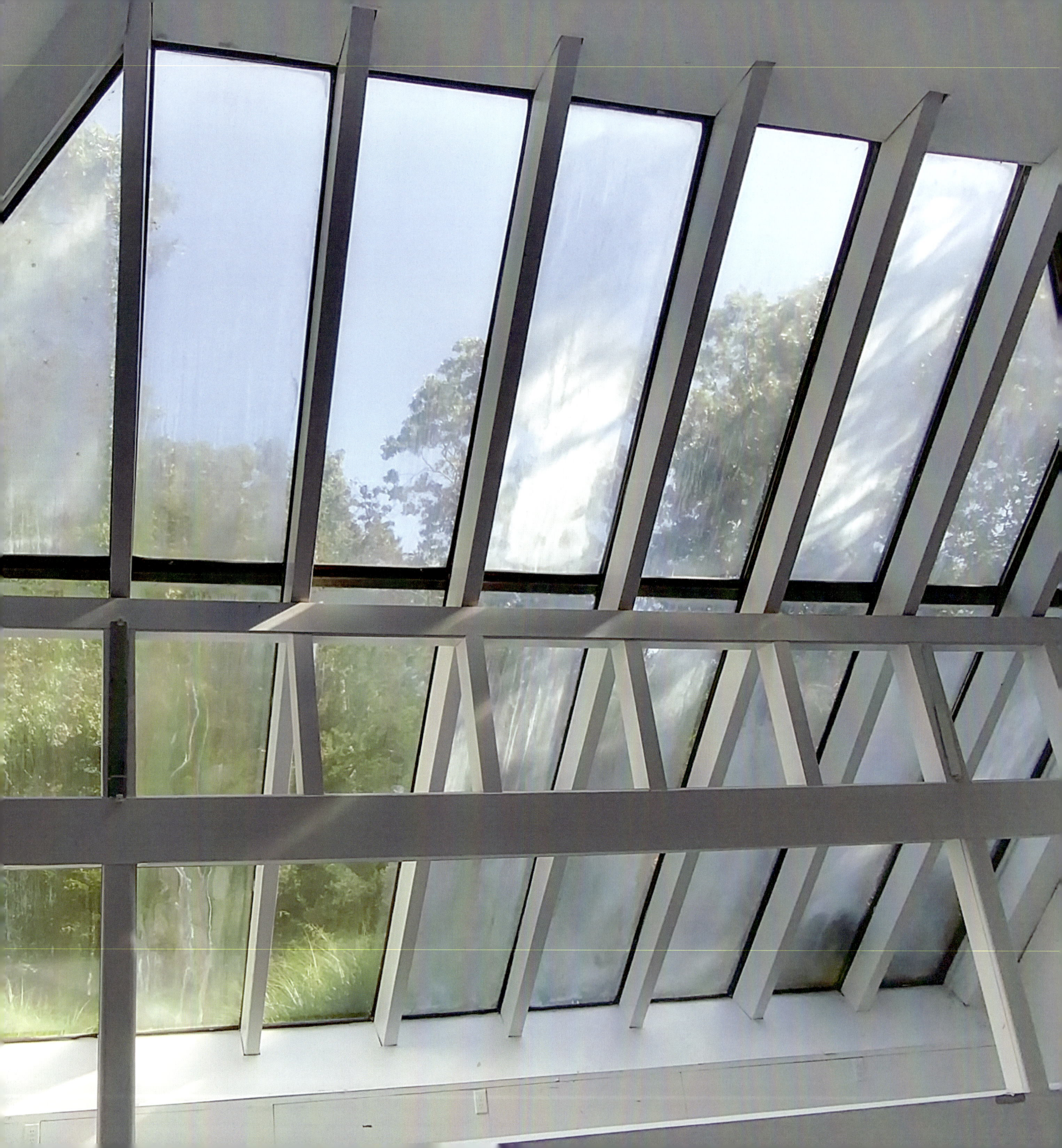

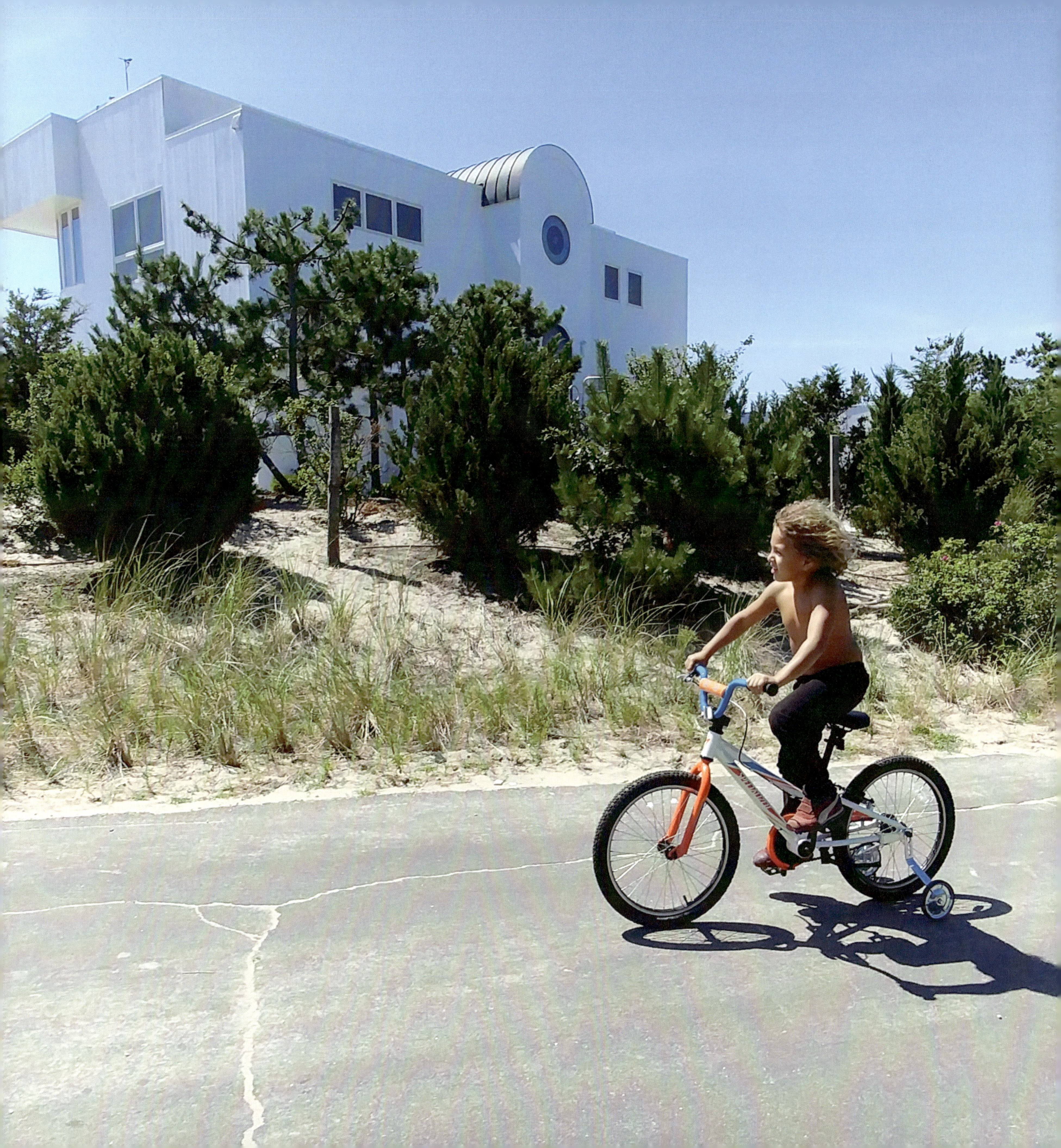

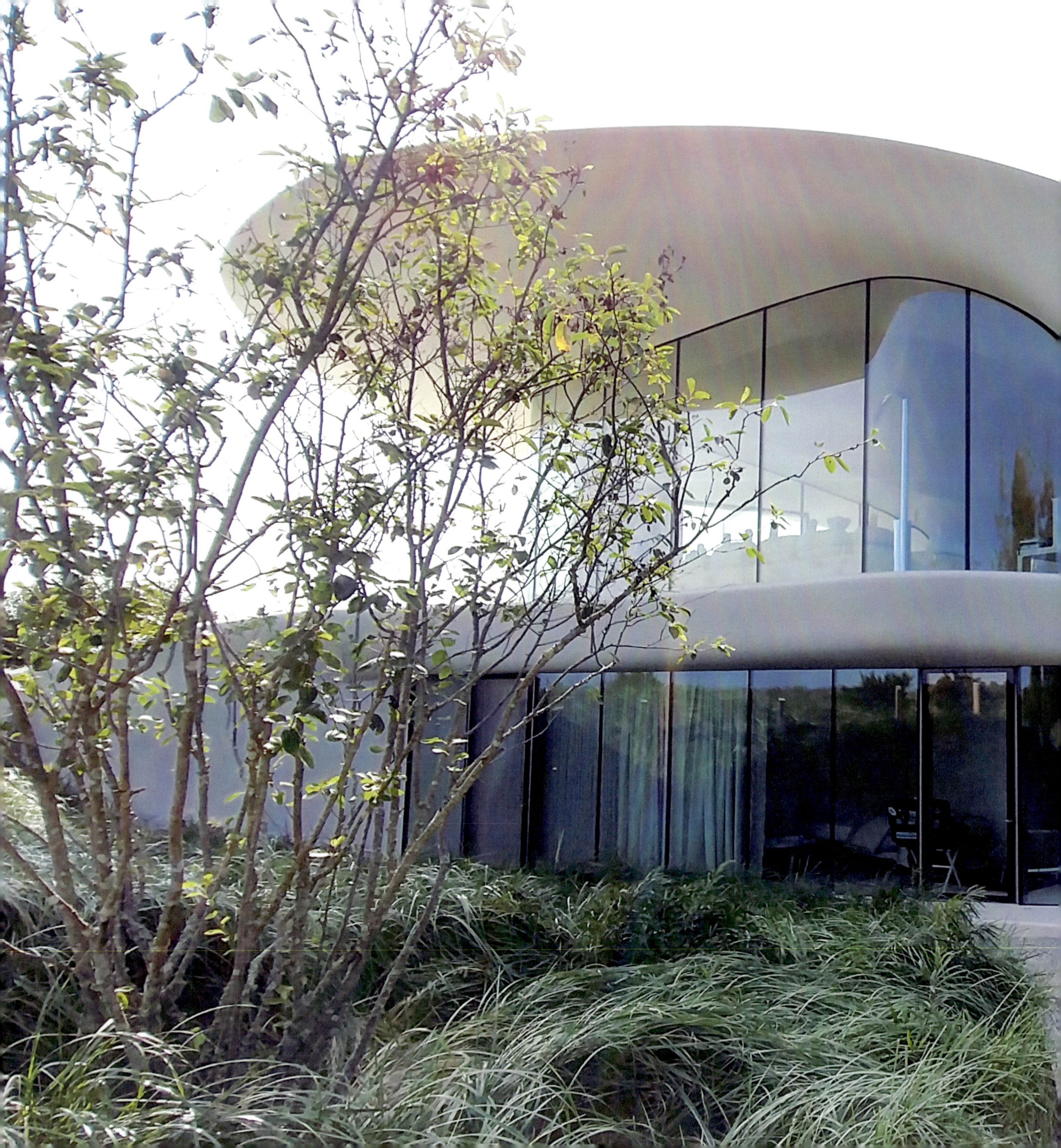

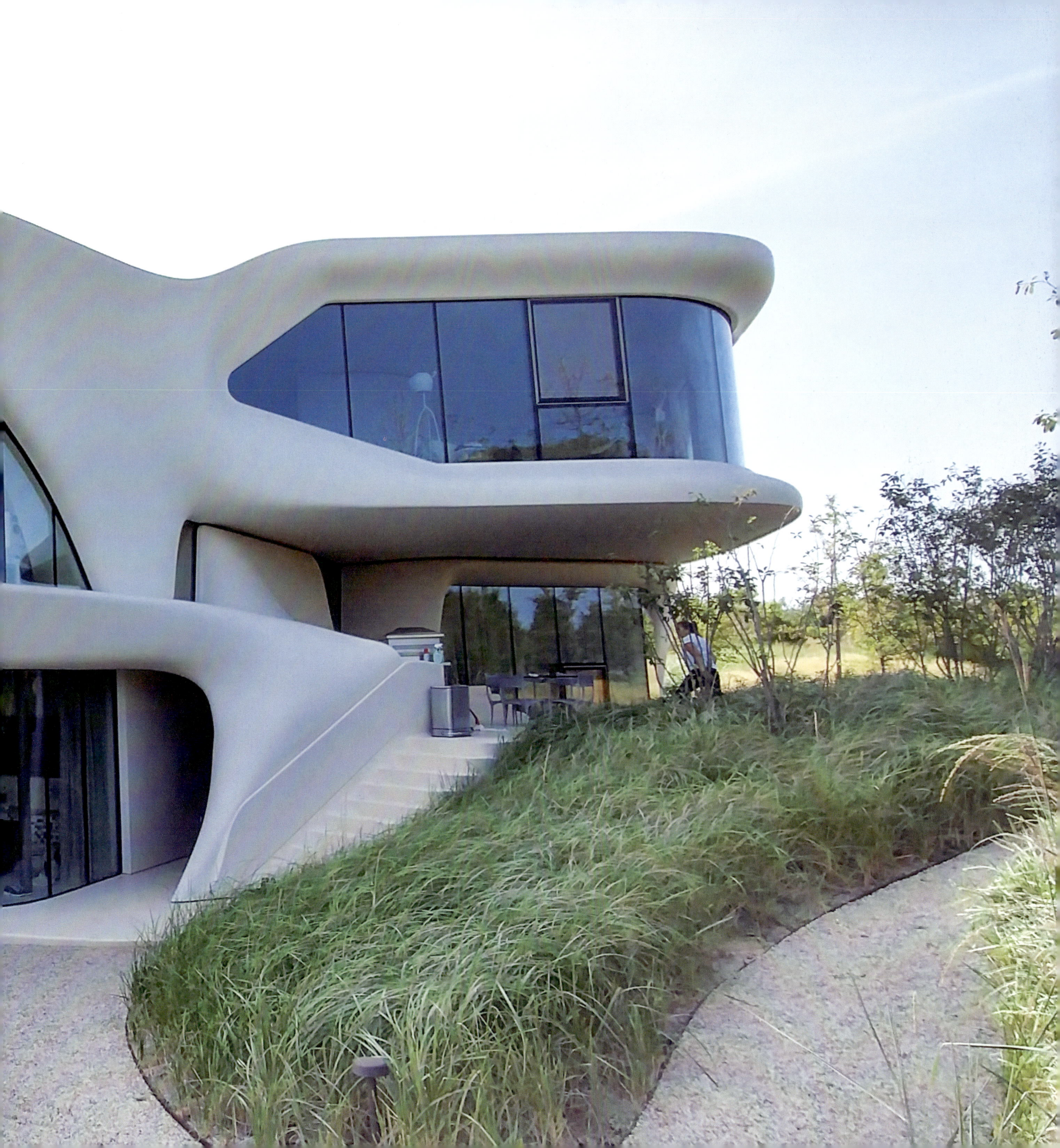

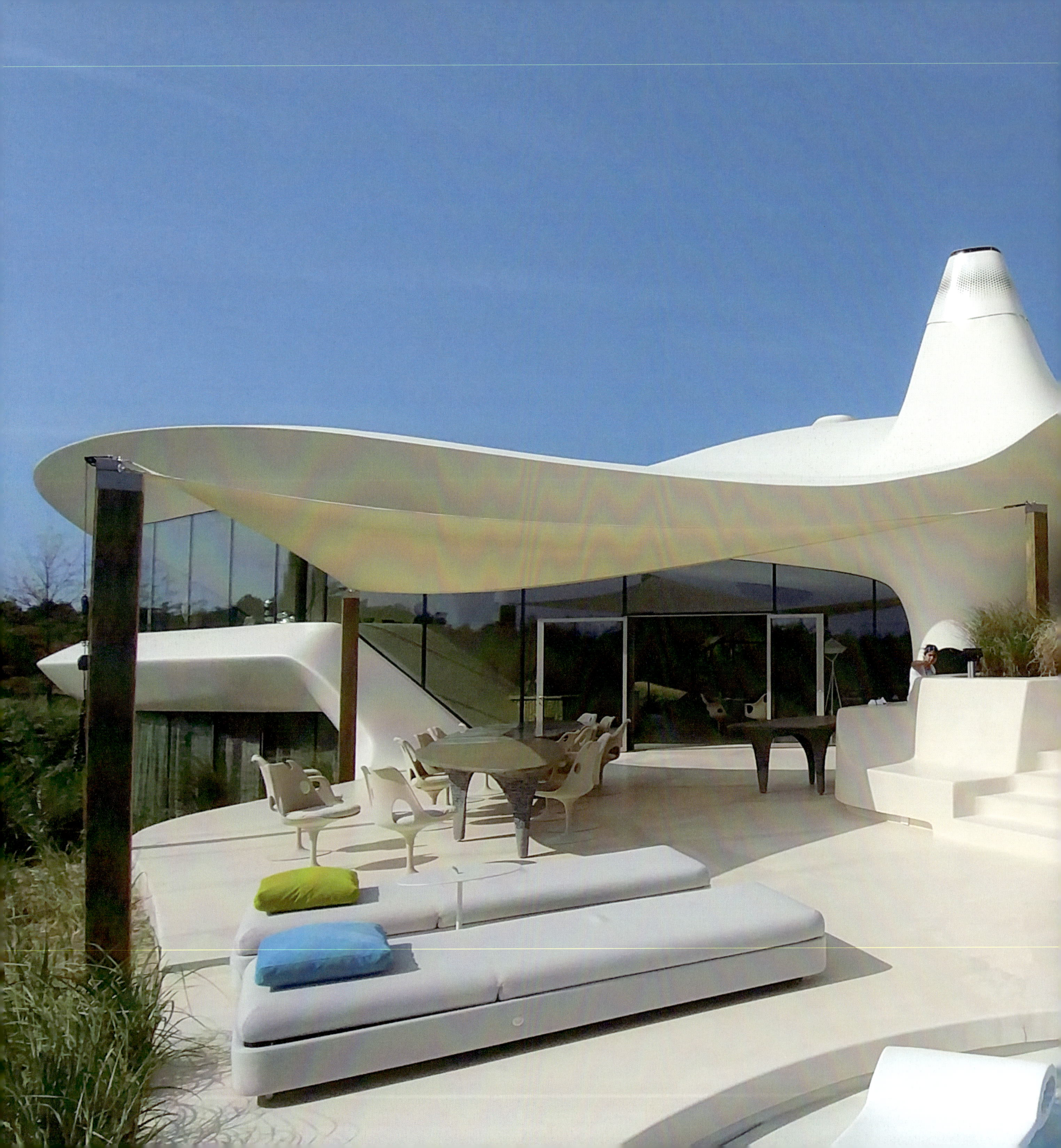

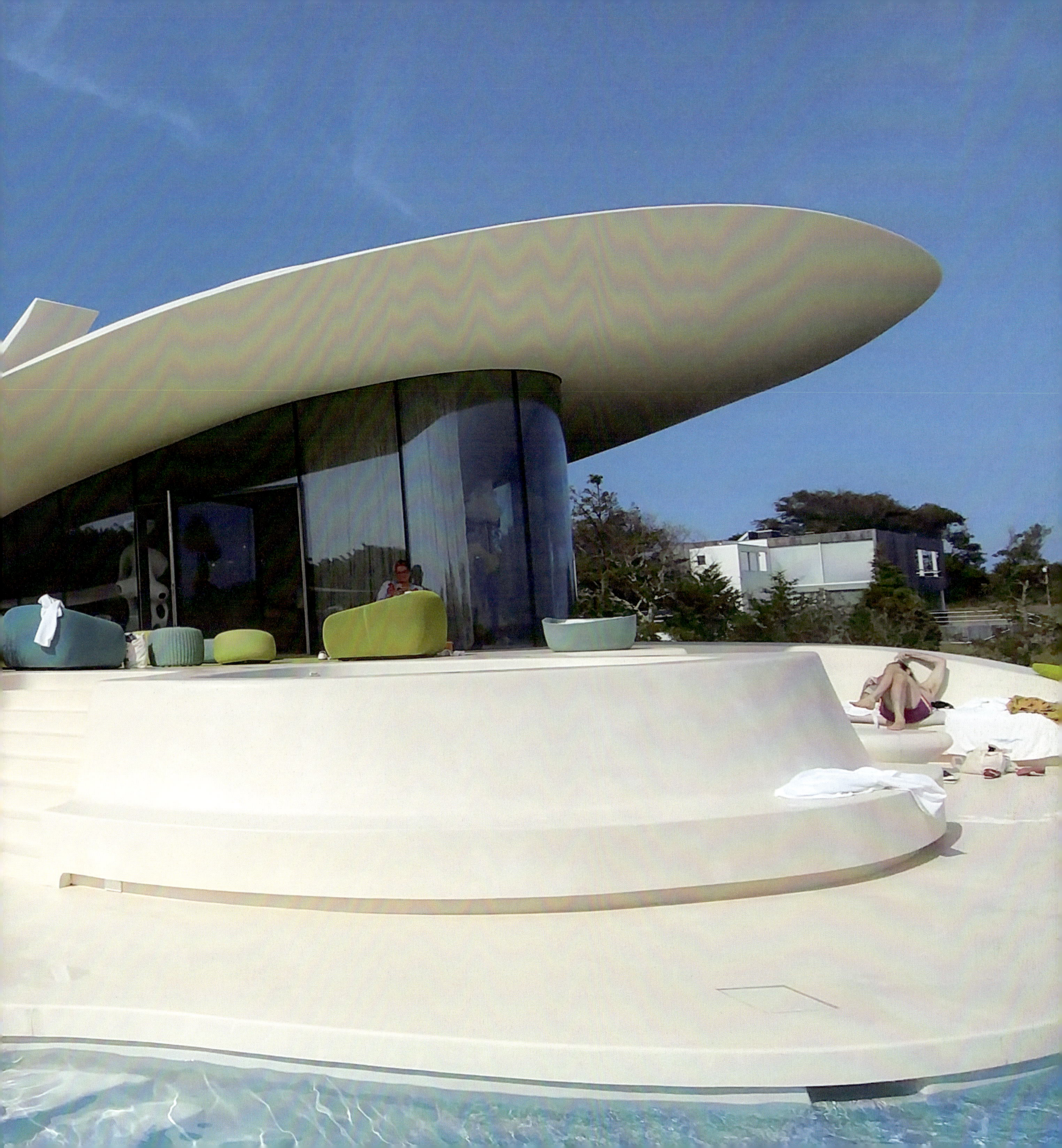

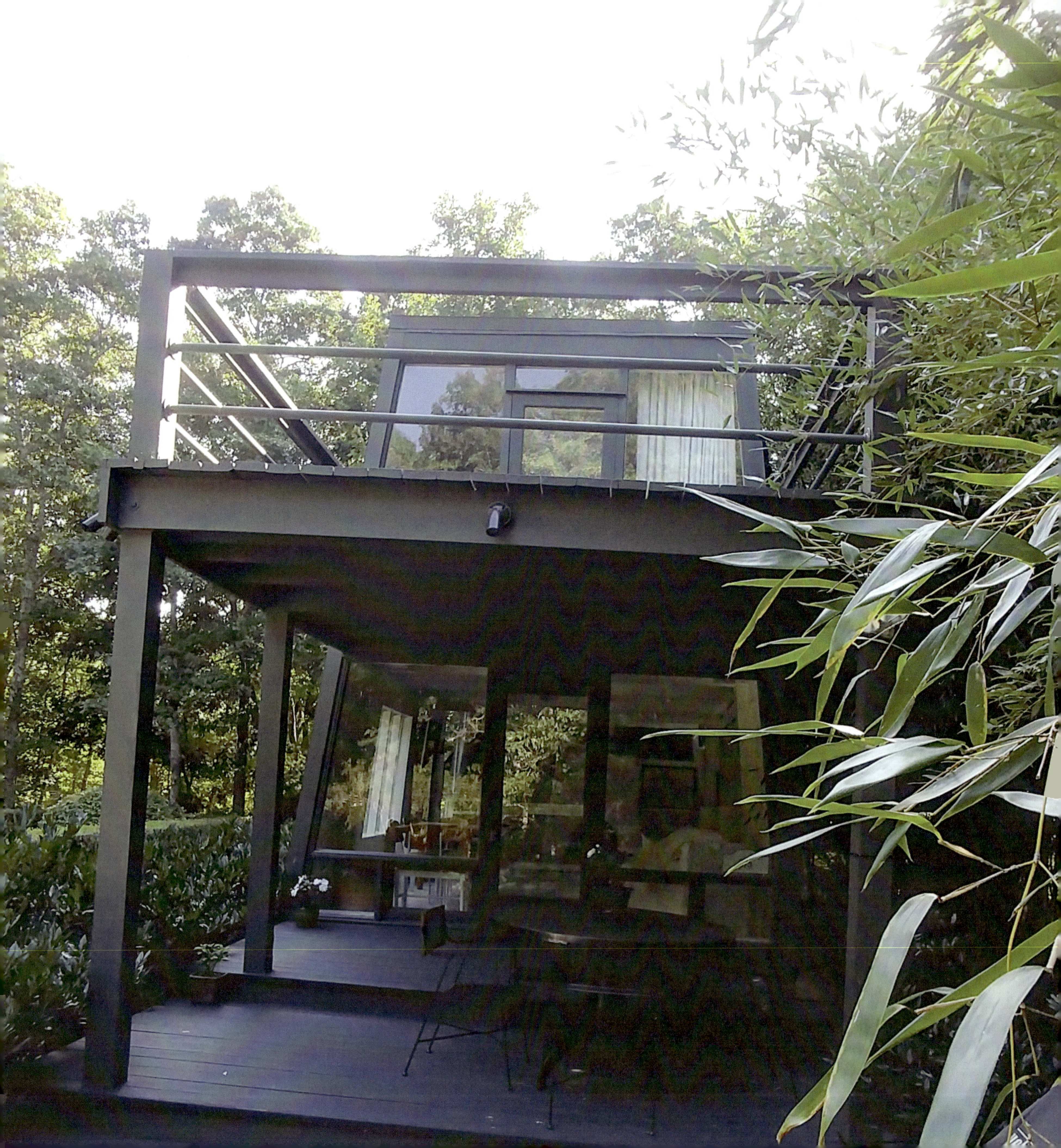

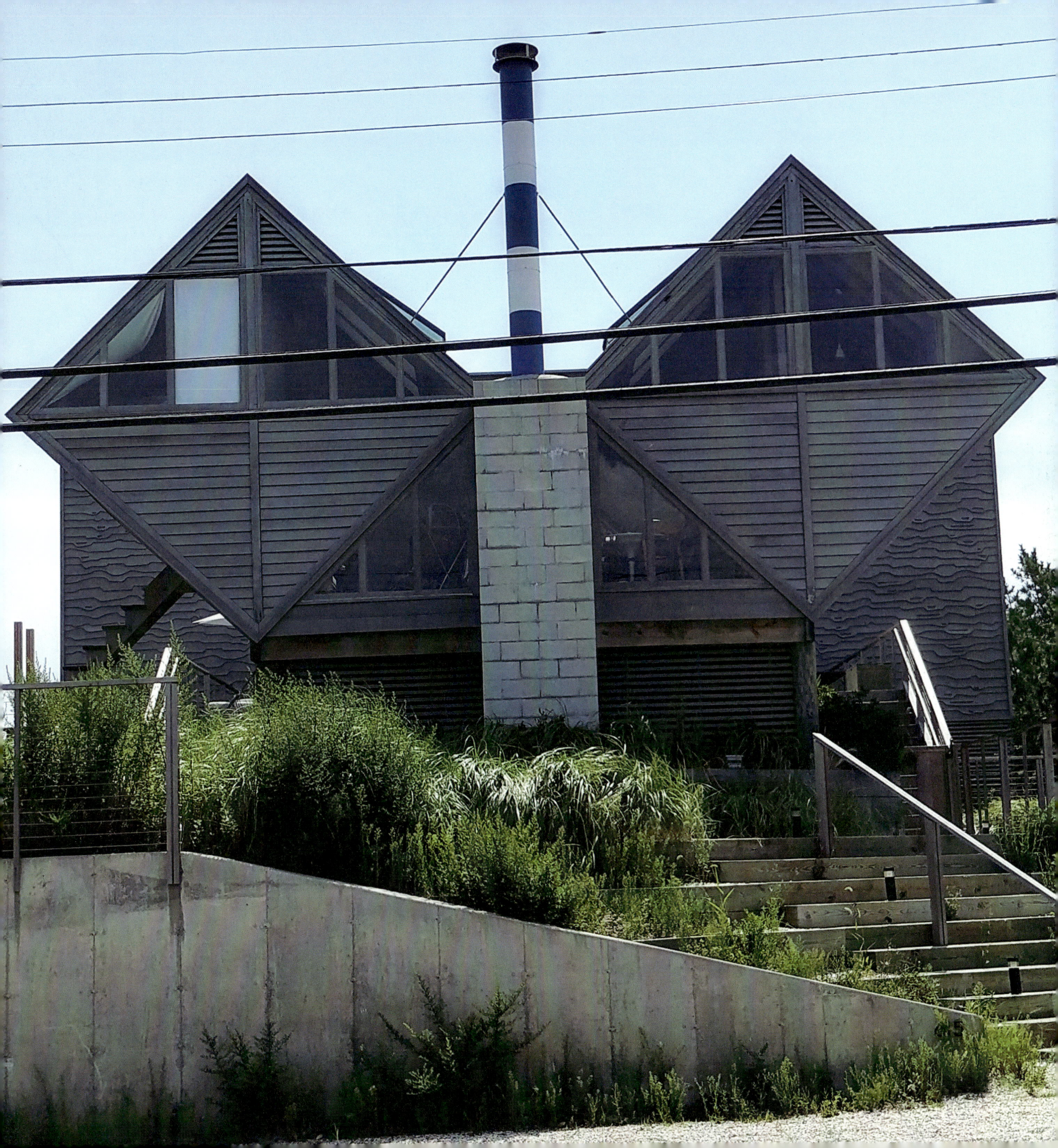

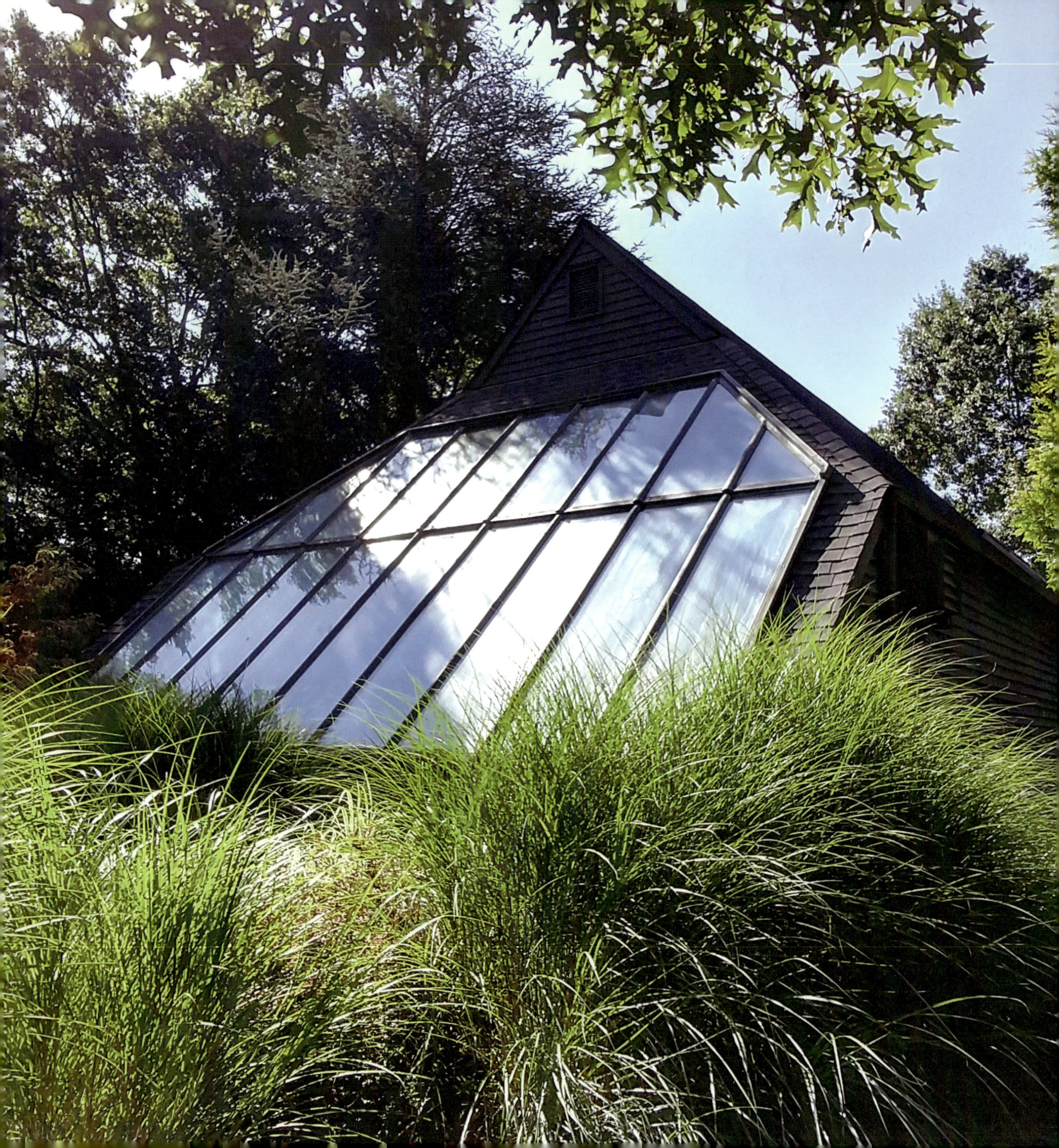

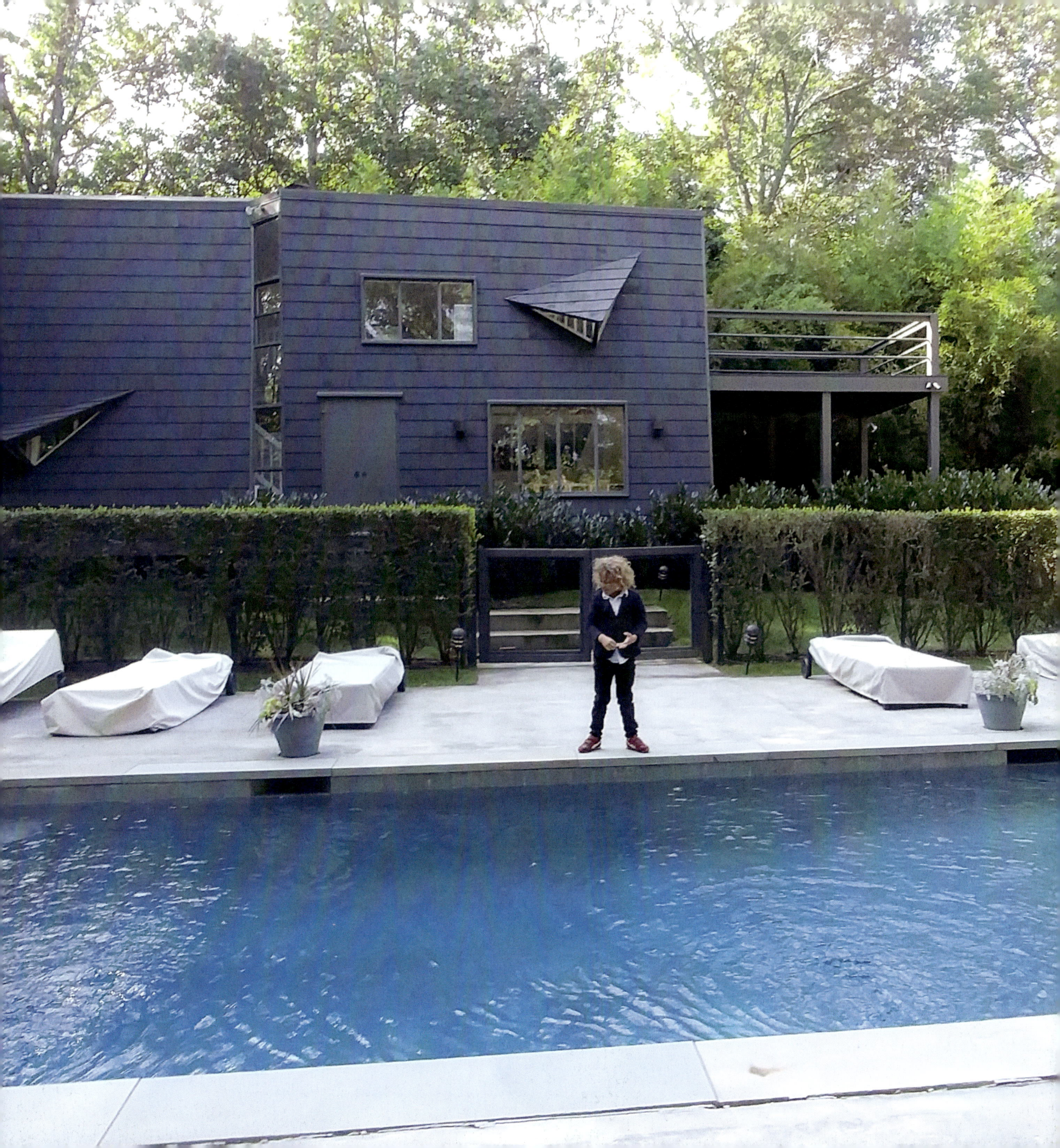

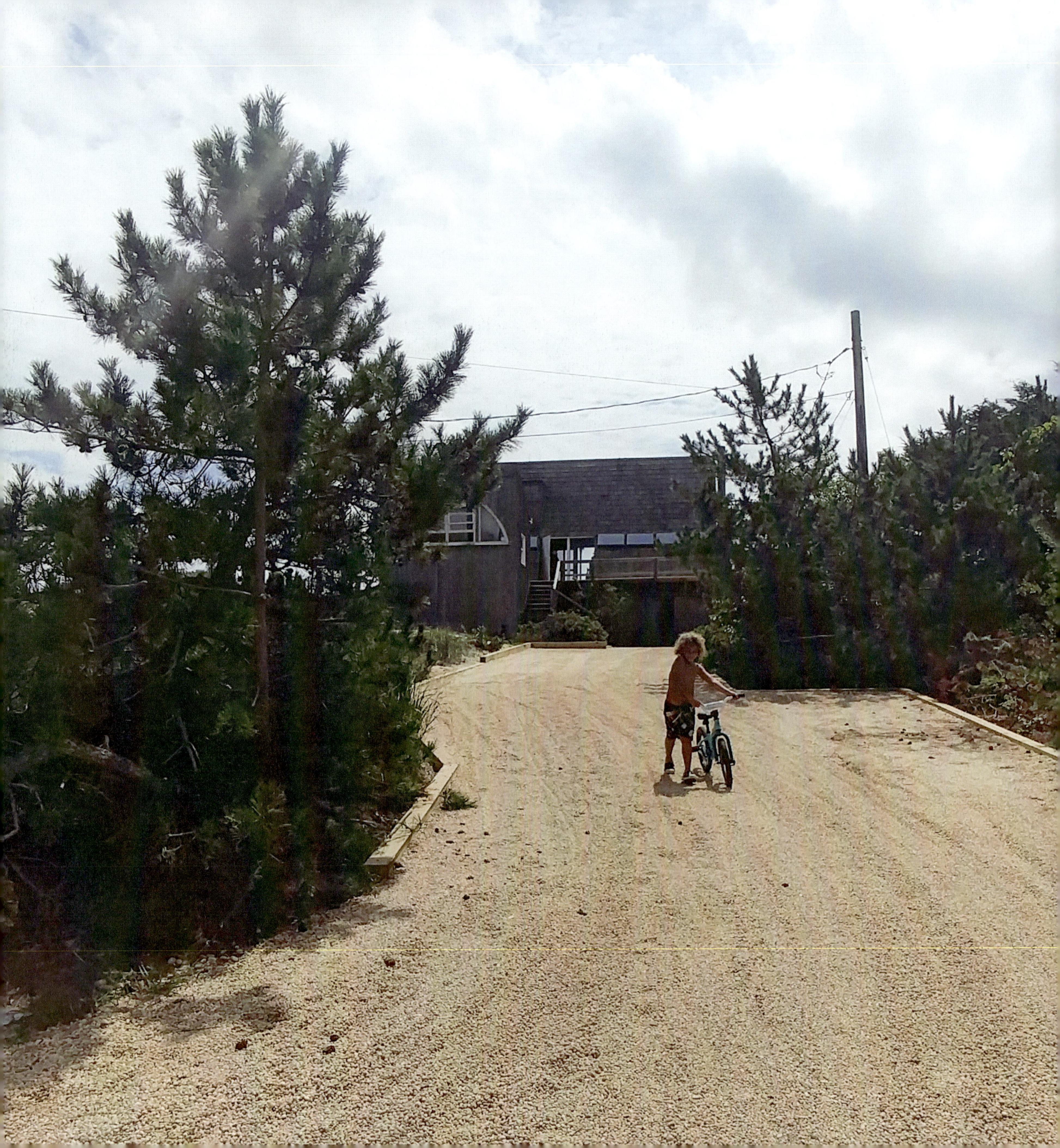

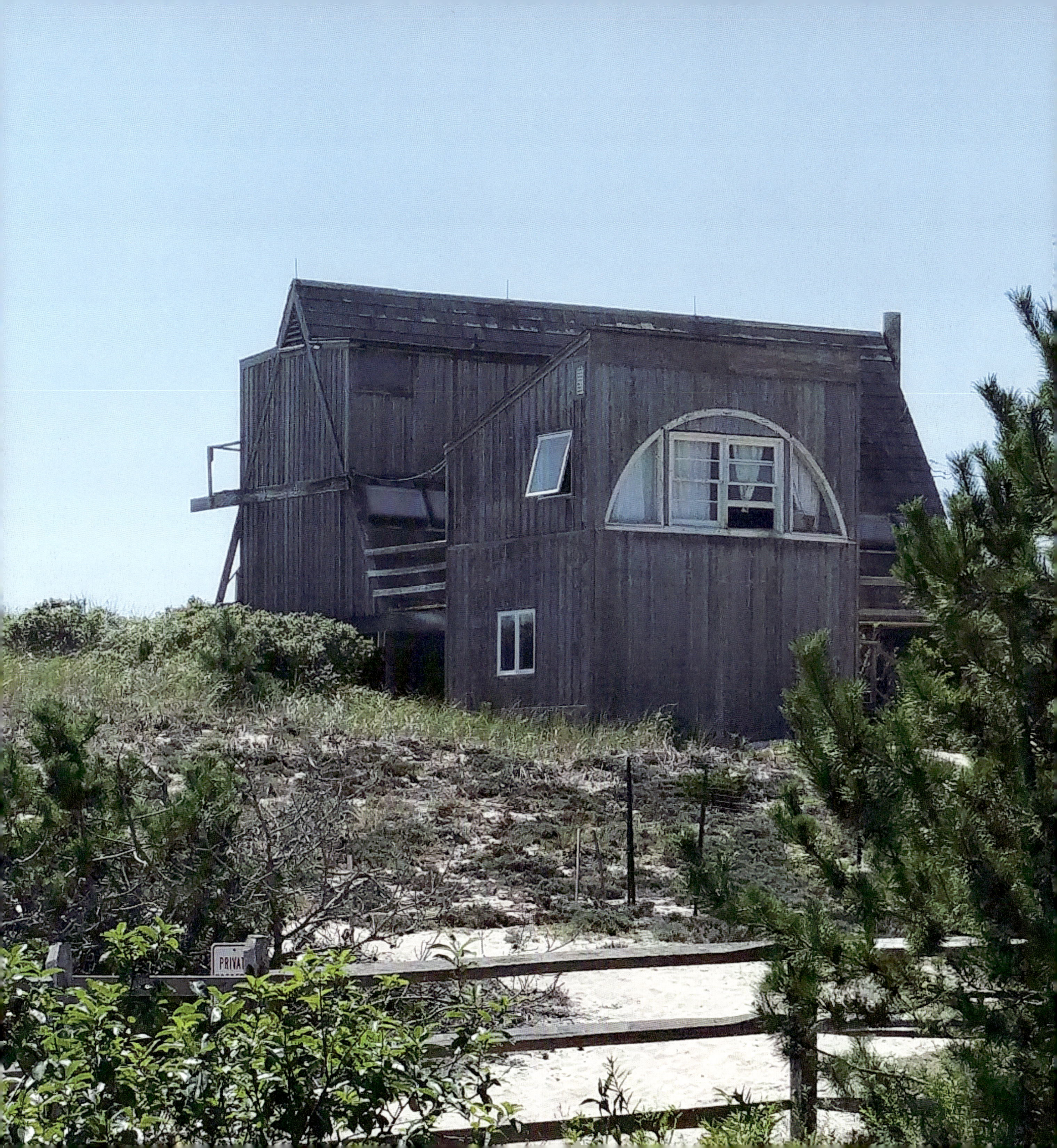

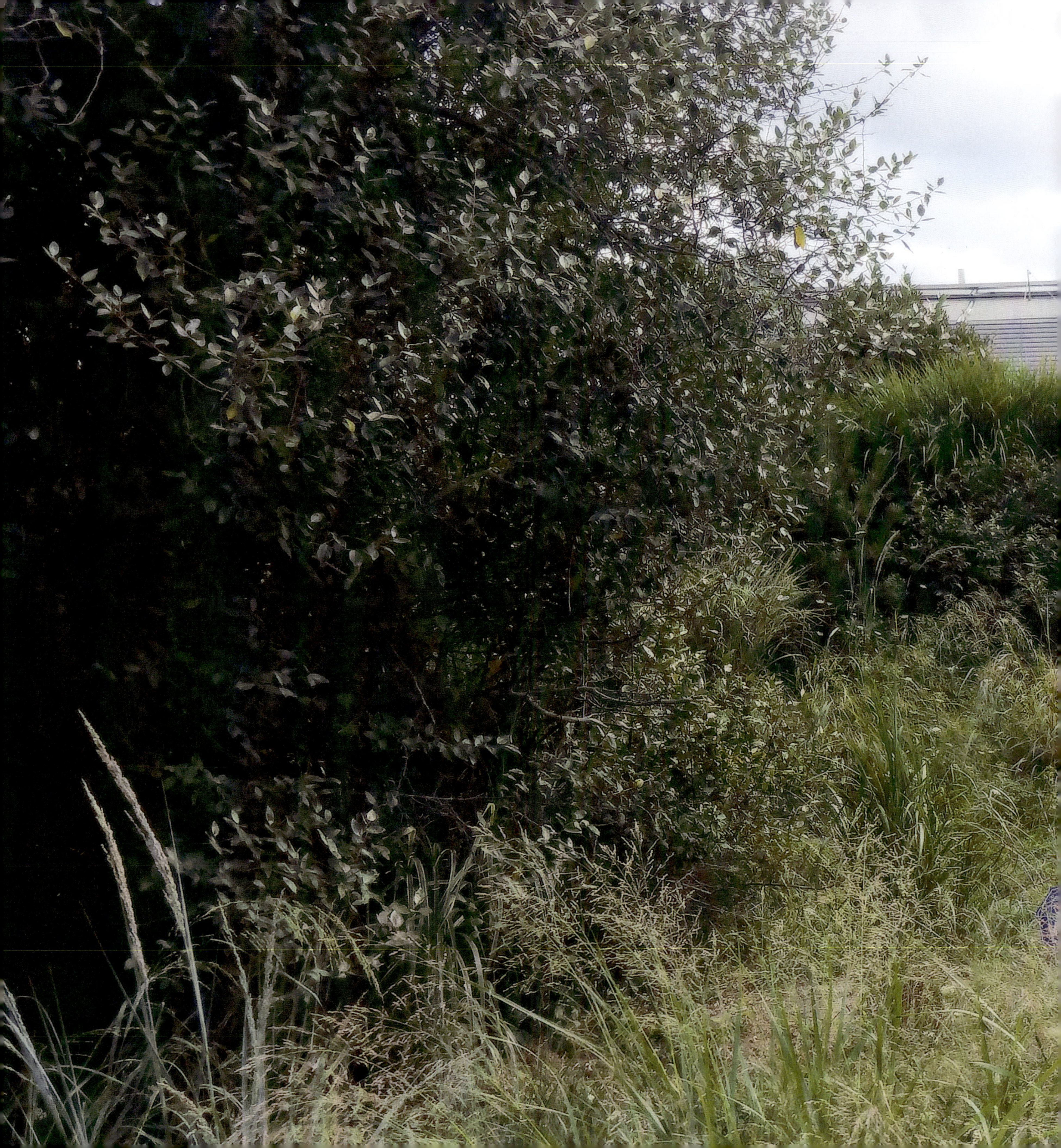

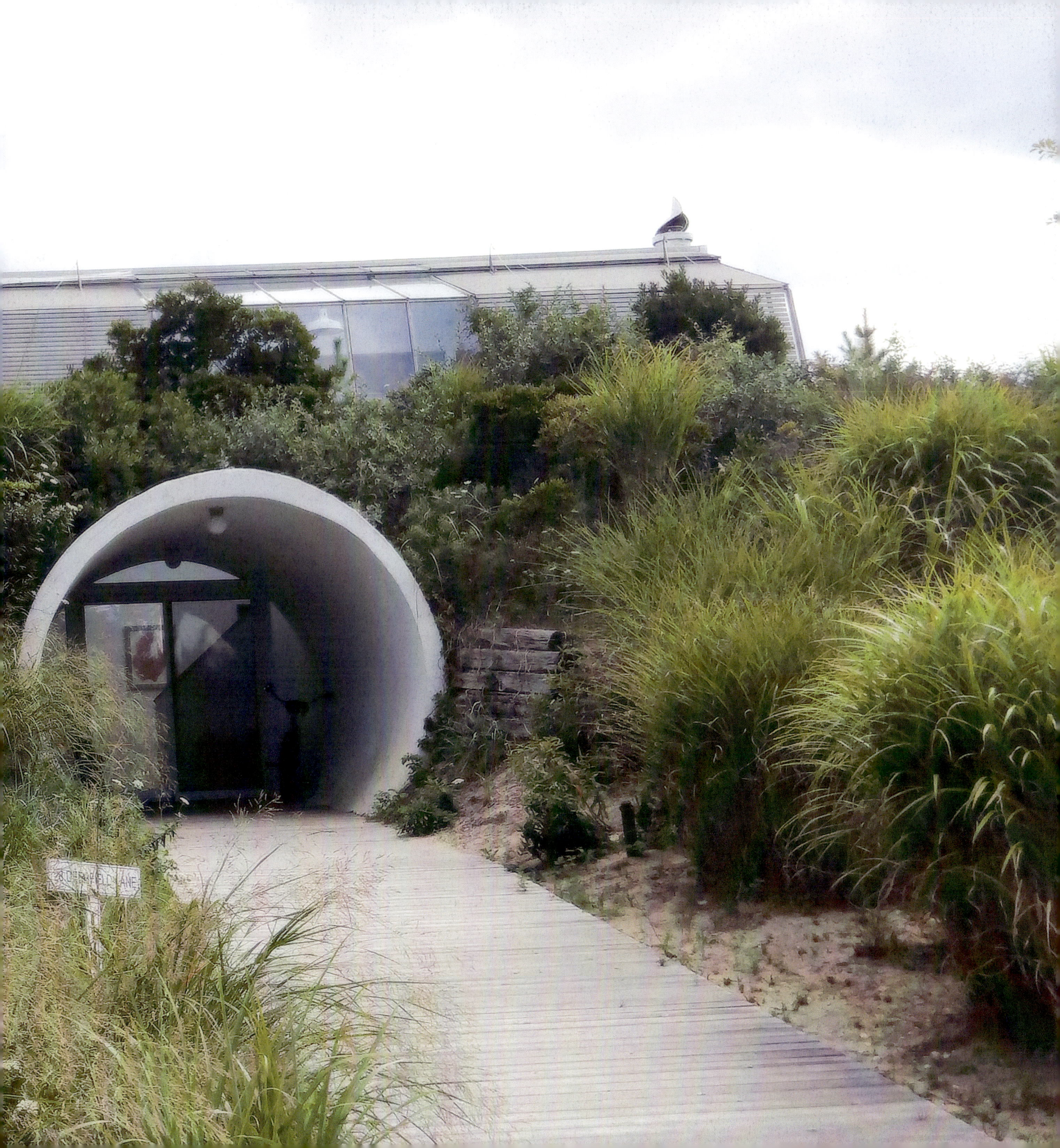

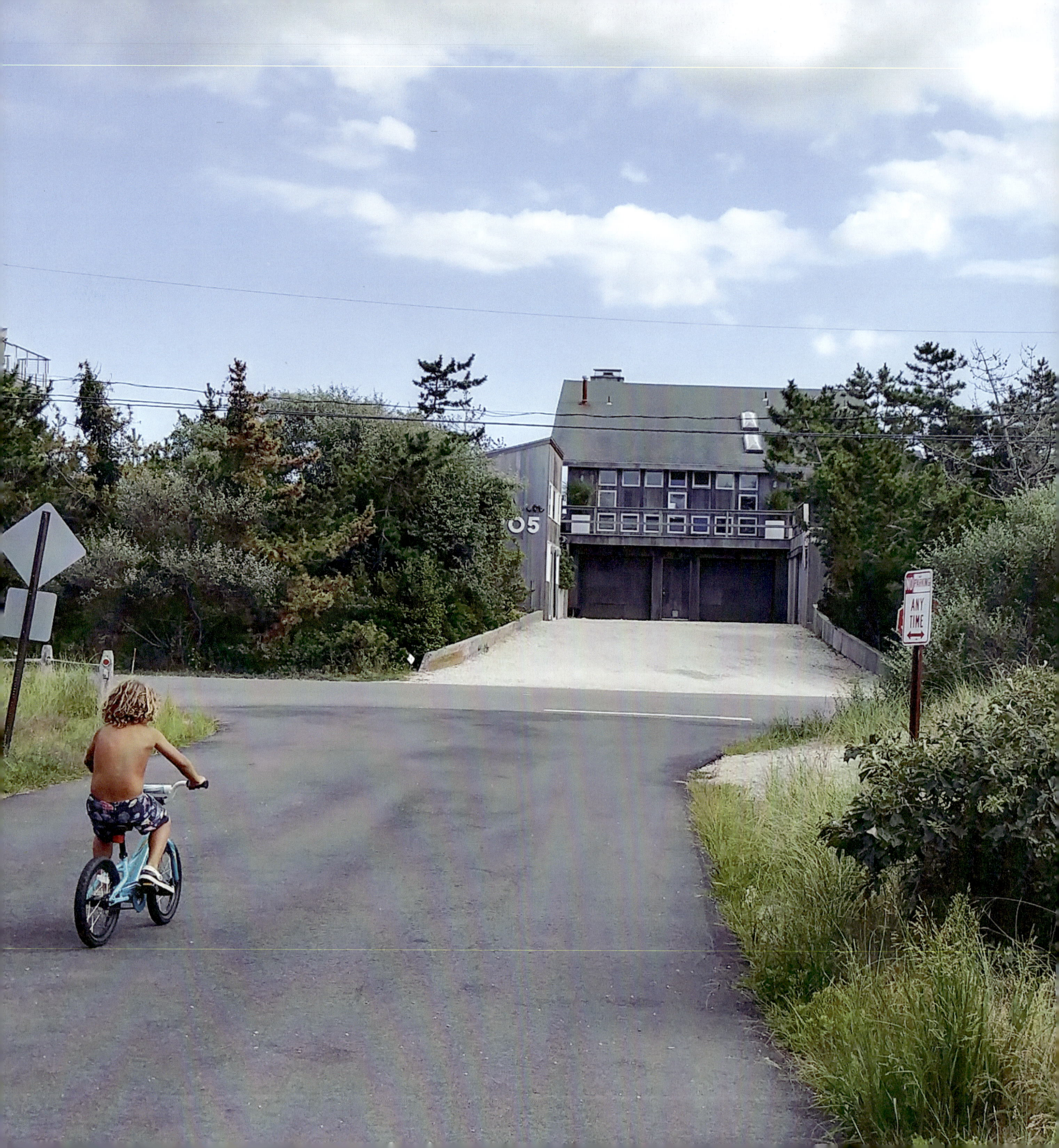

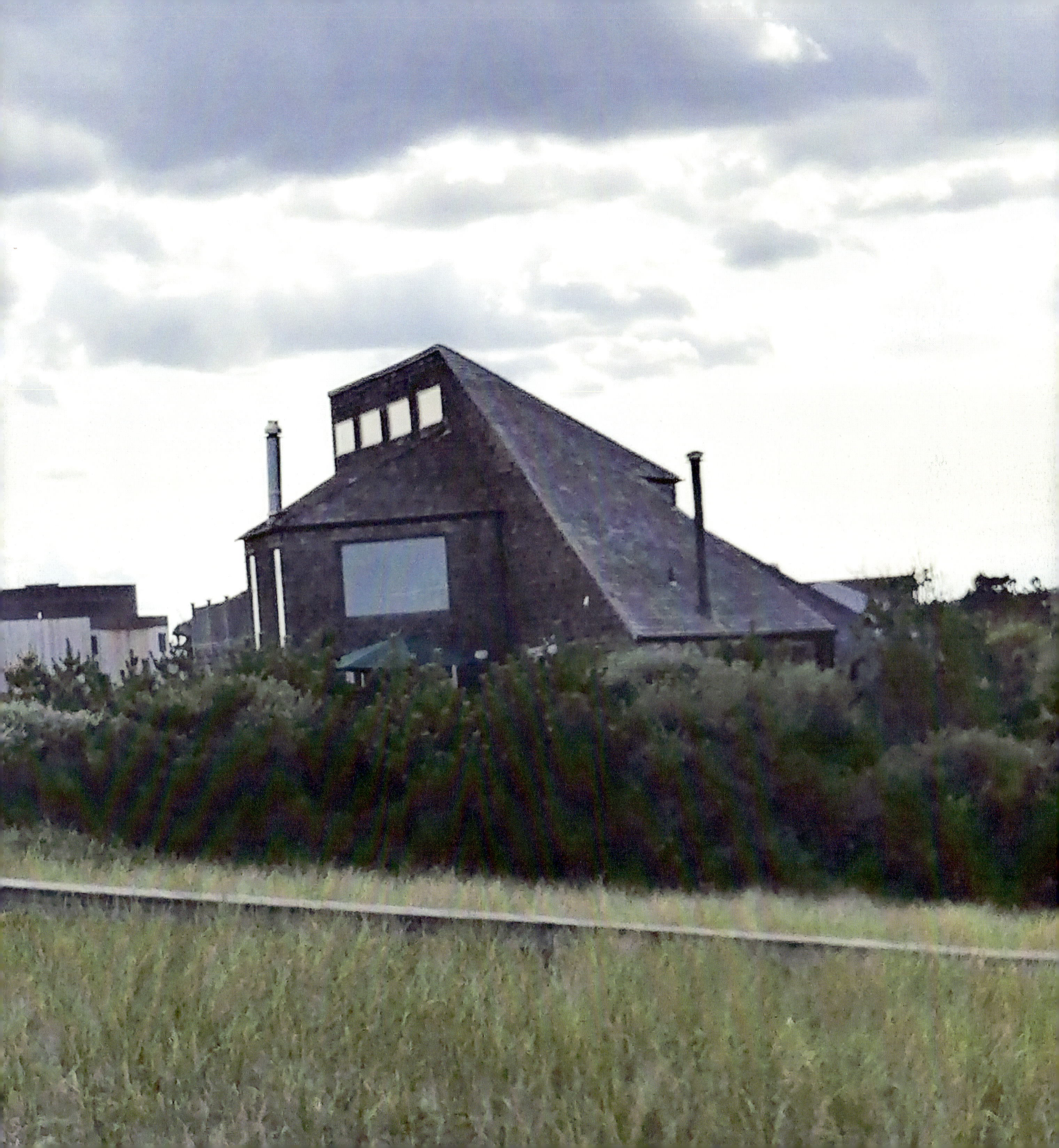

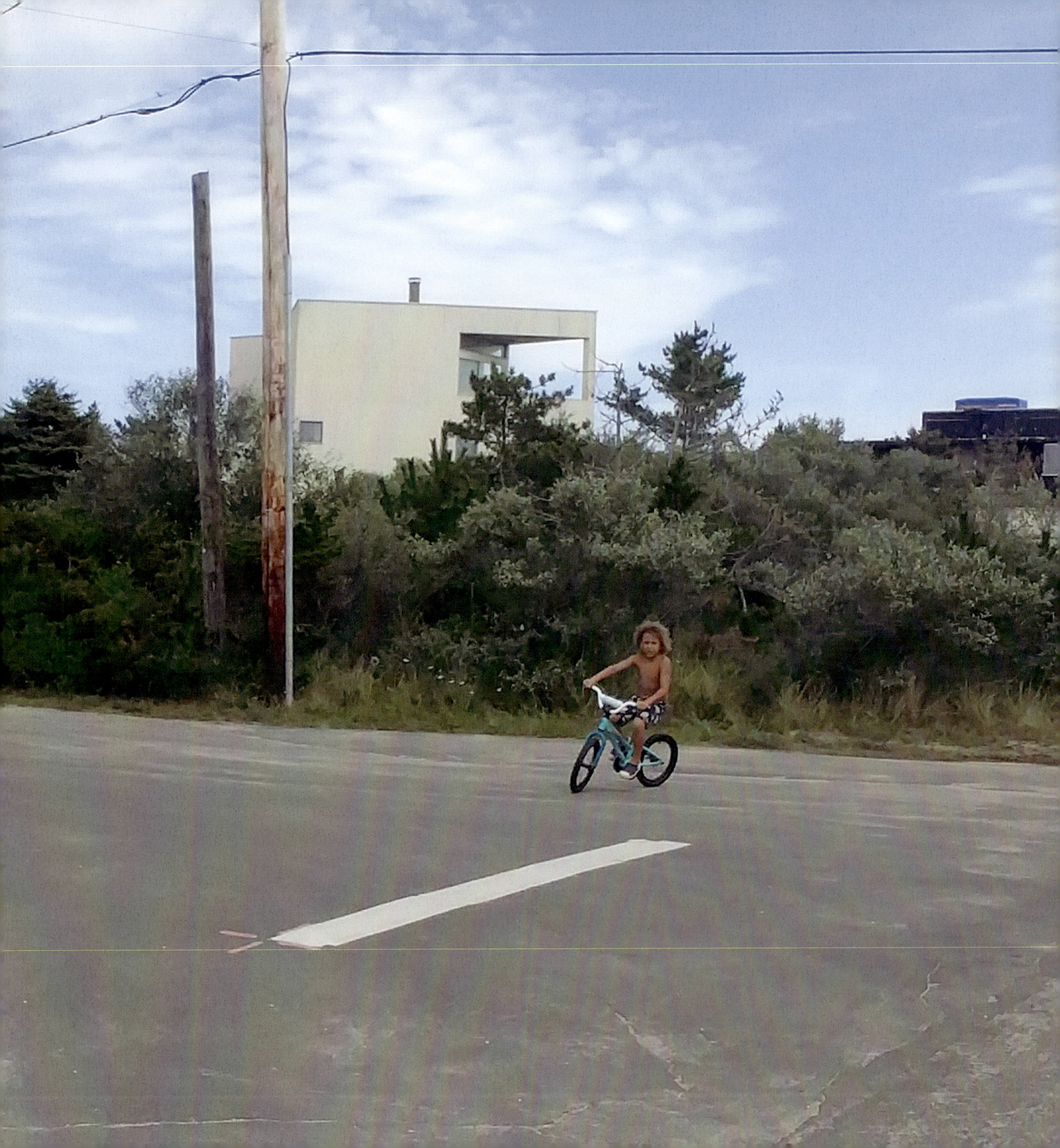

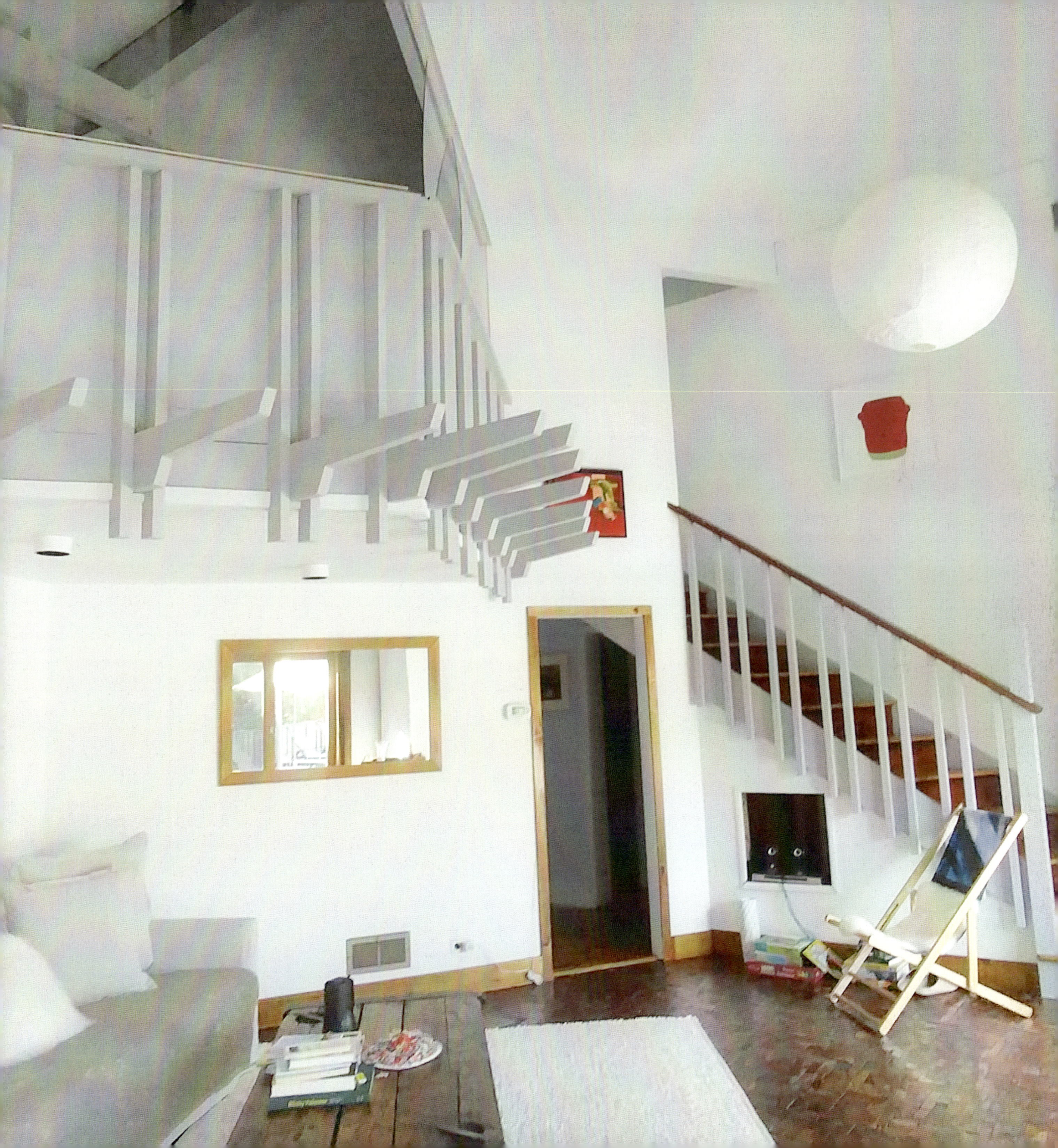

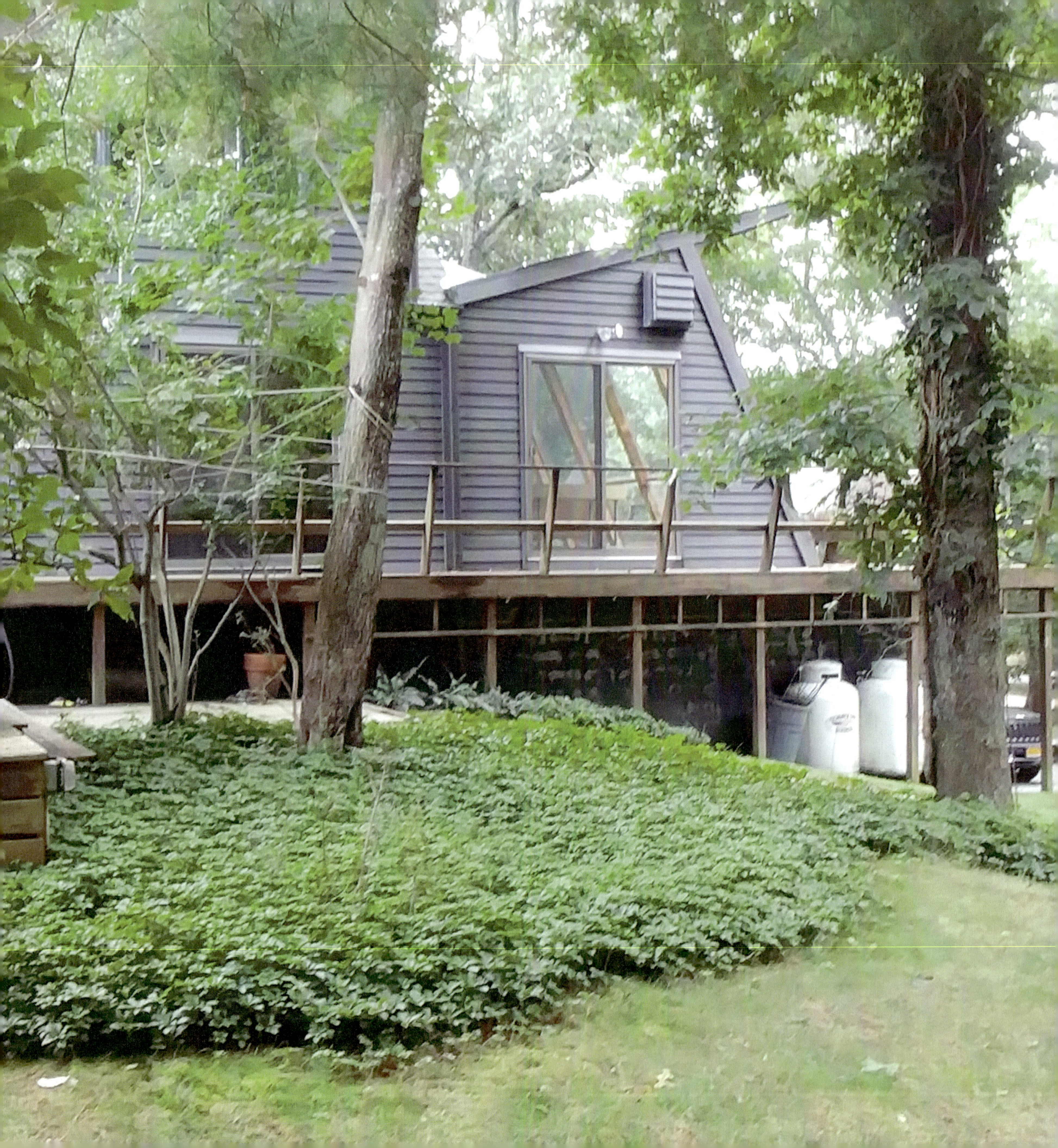

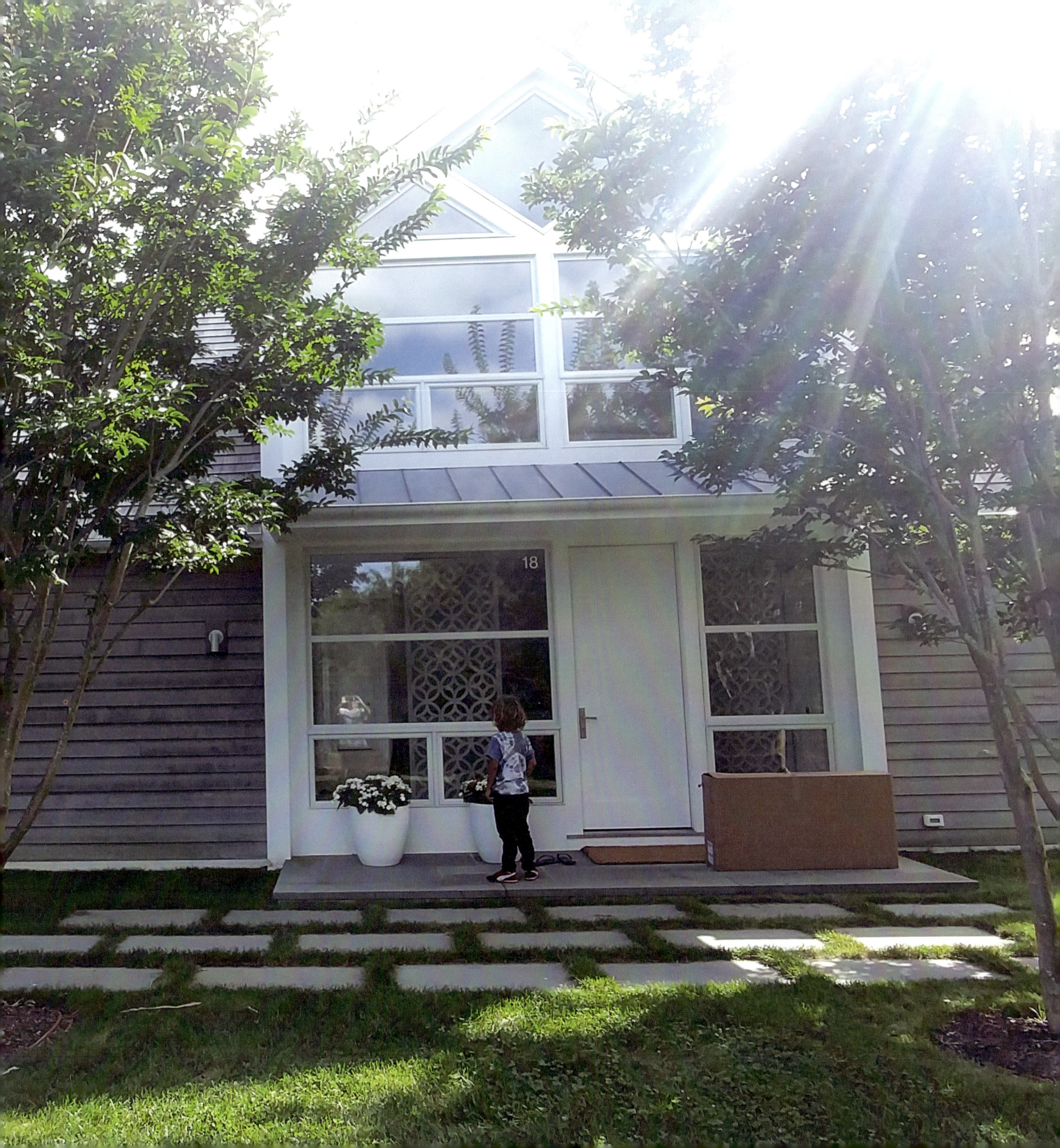

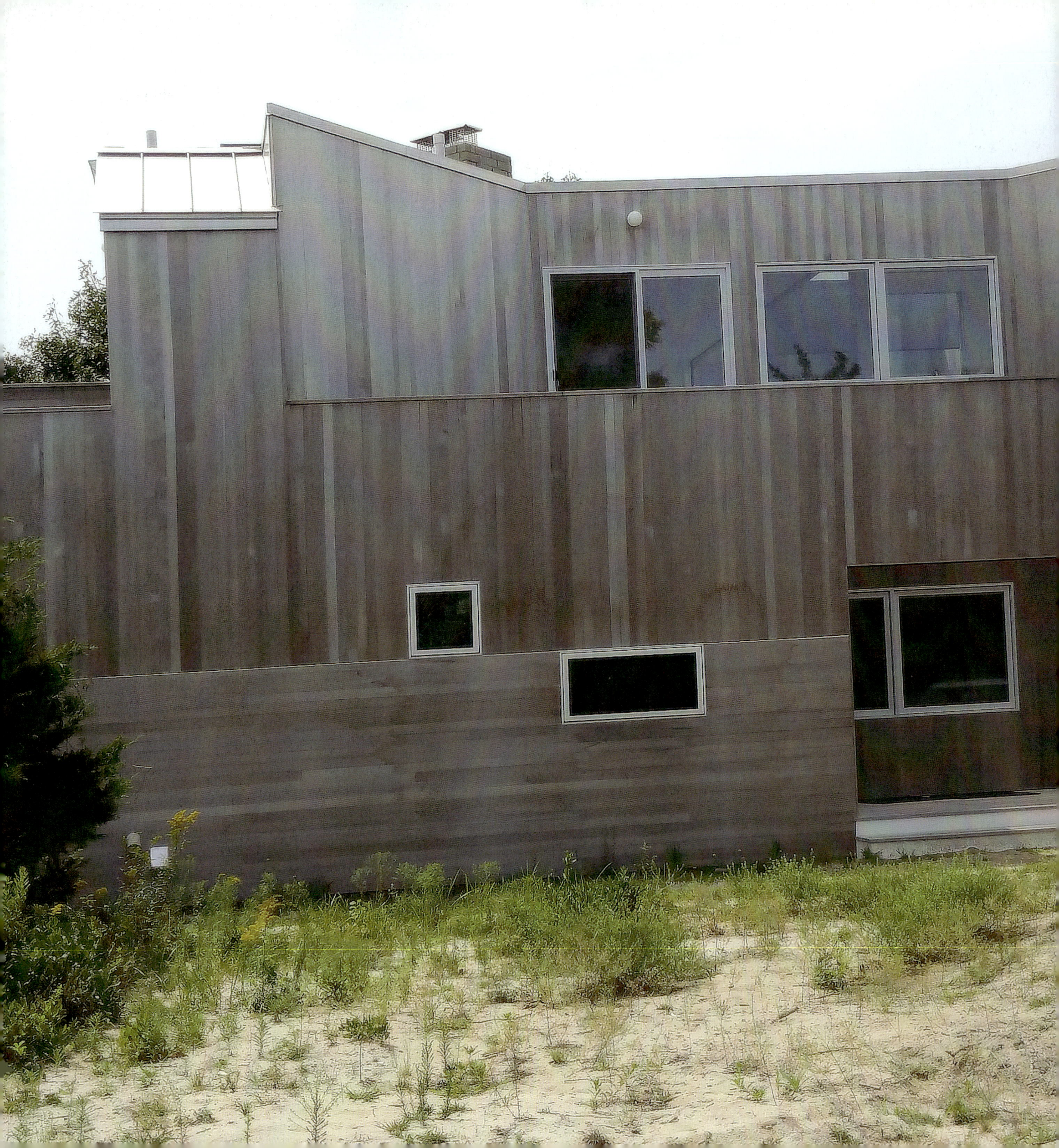

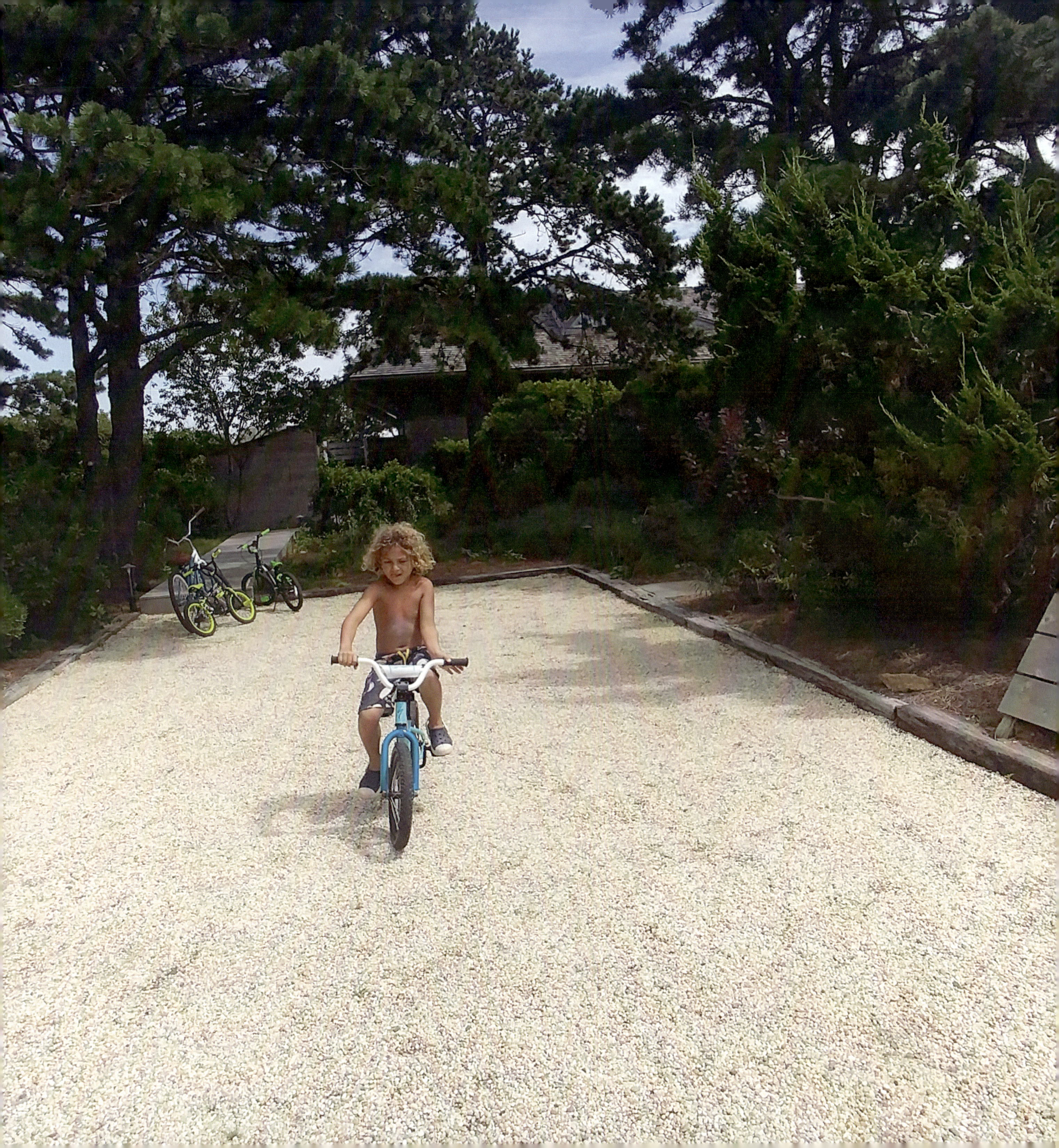

Dunes

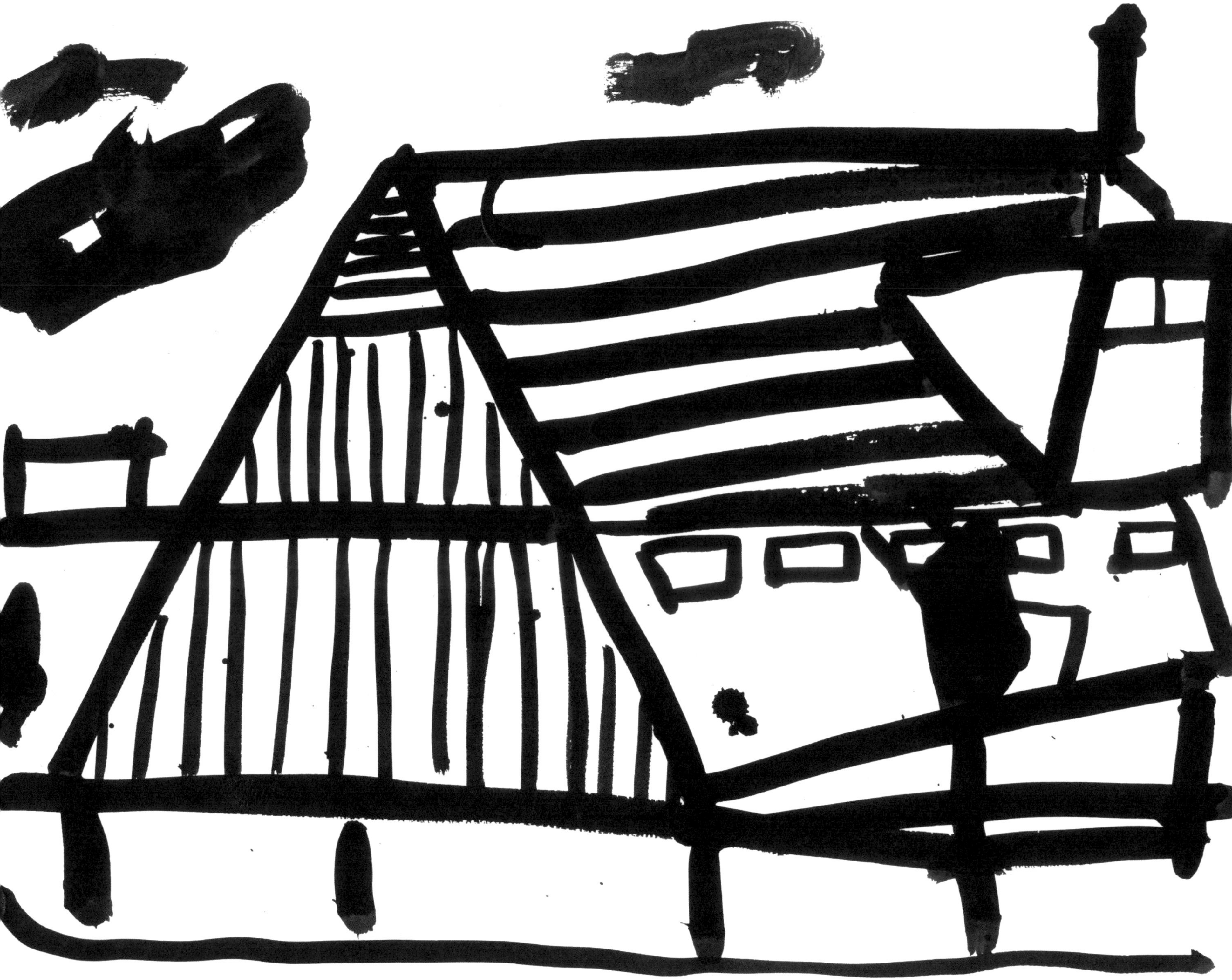

Dunes

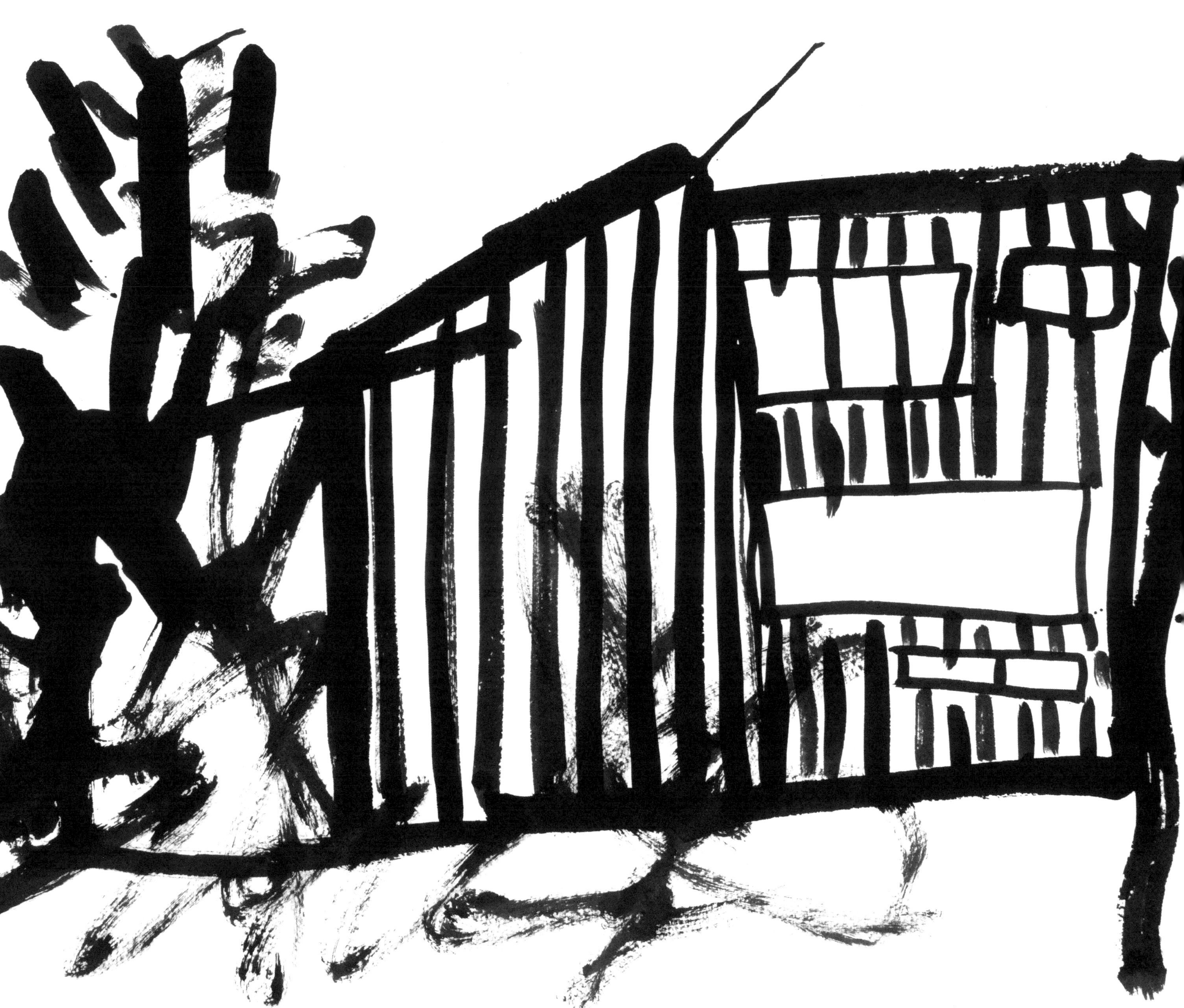

Andrew Geller, Sag Harbor

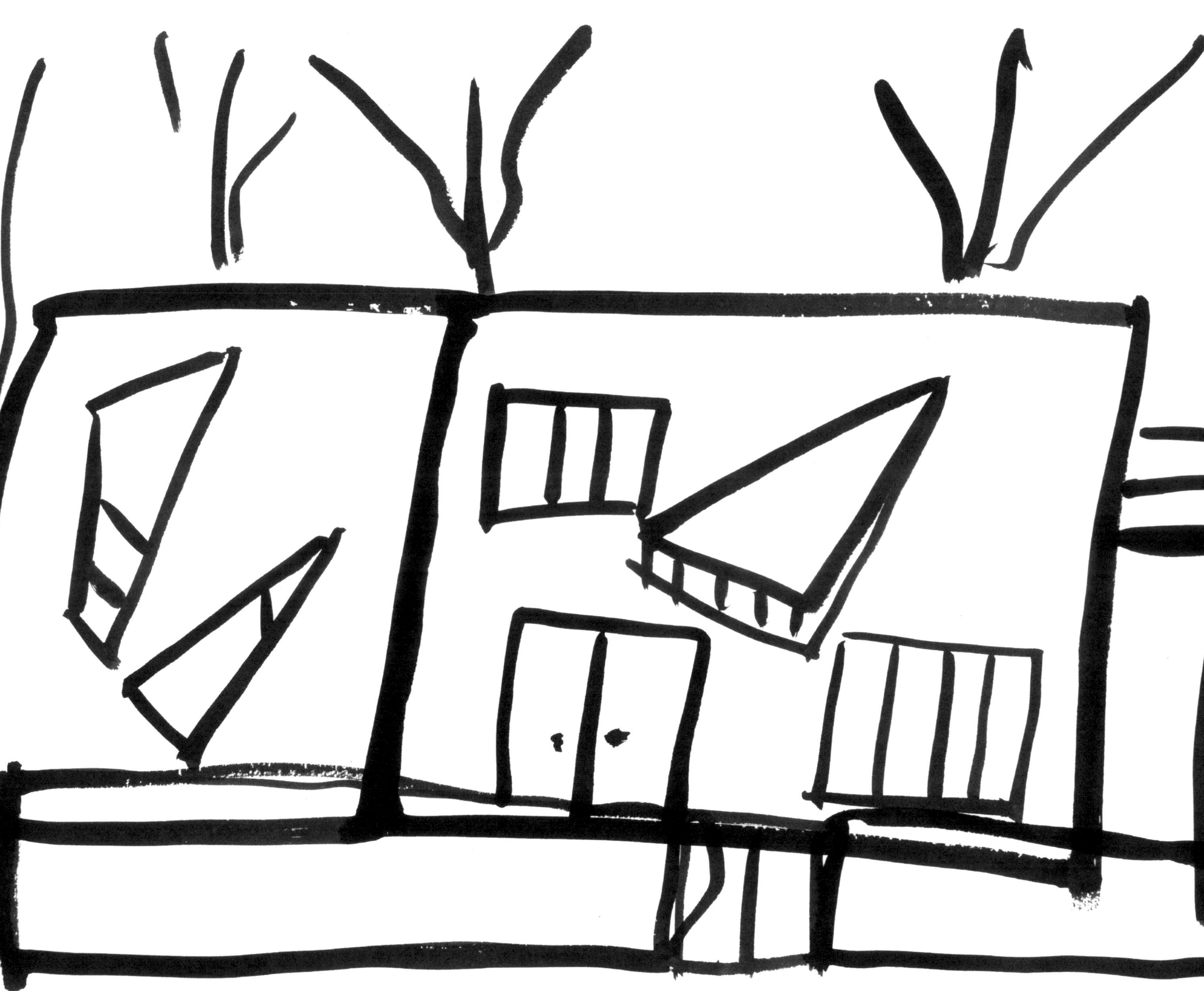

Diller Scofidio + Renfro, Amagansett

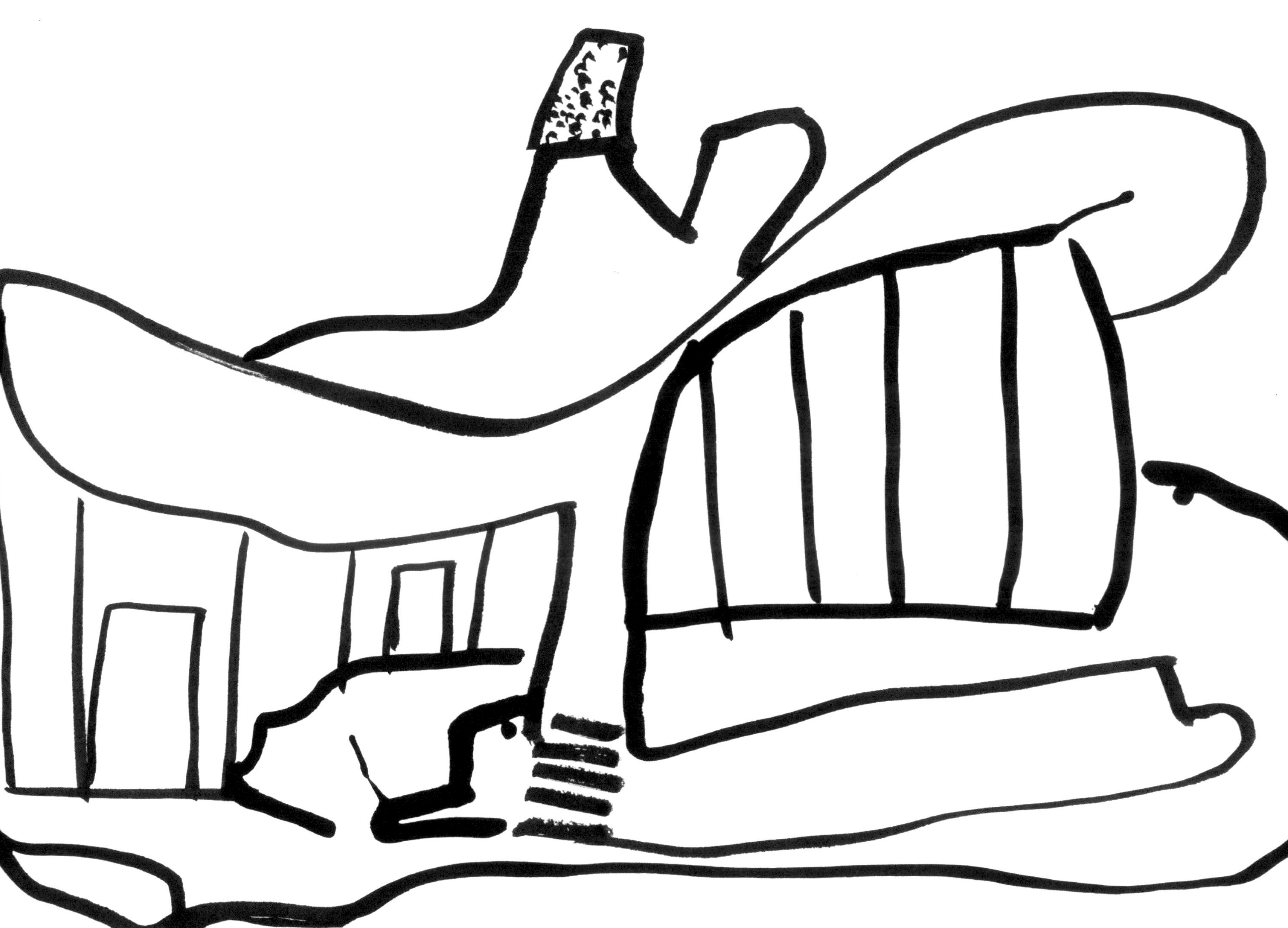

Andrew Geller, Dunes

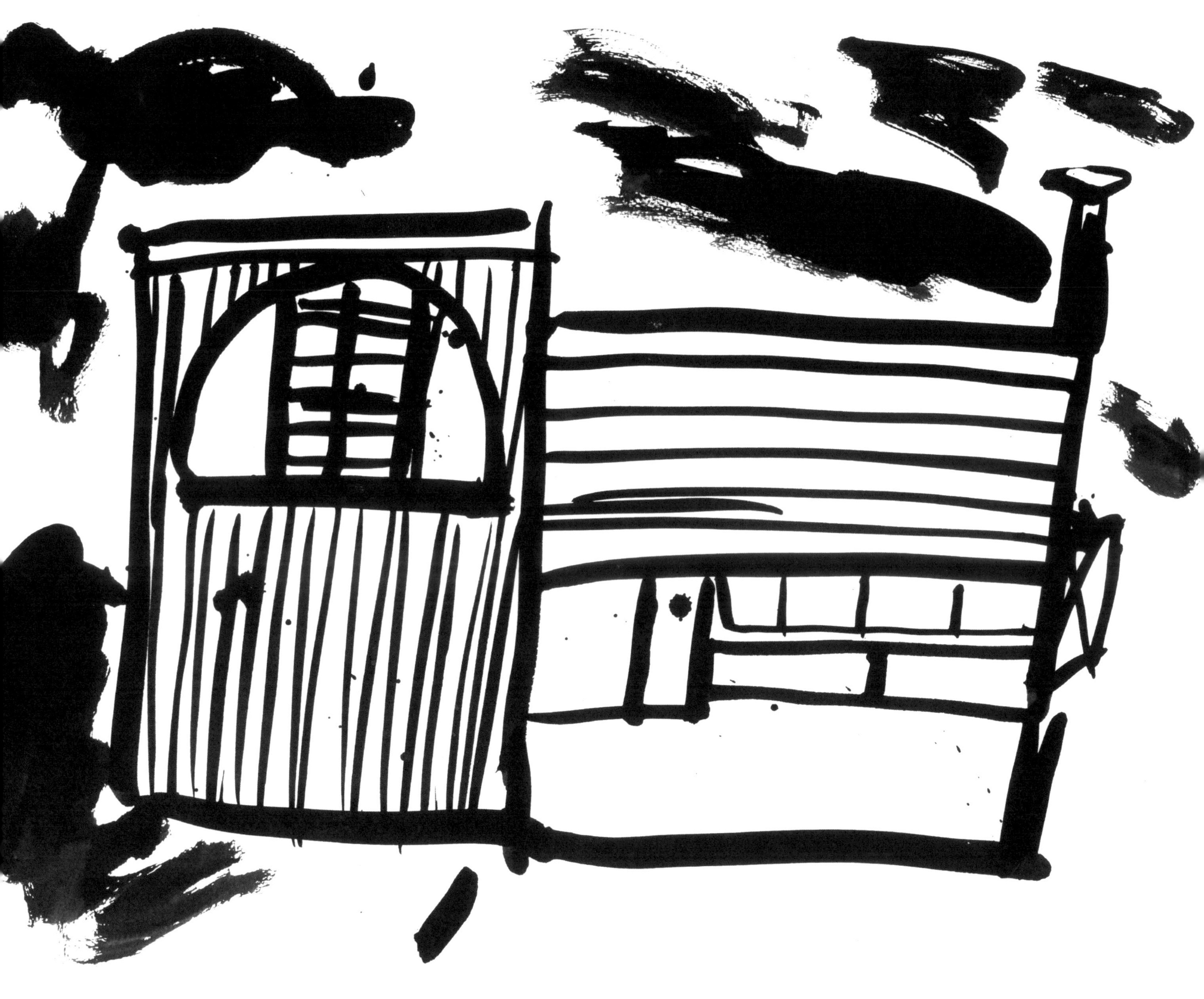

Sag Harbor

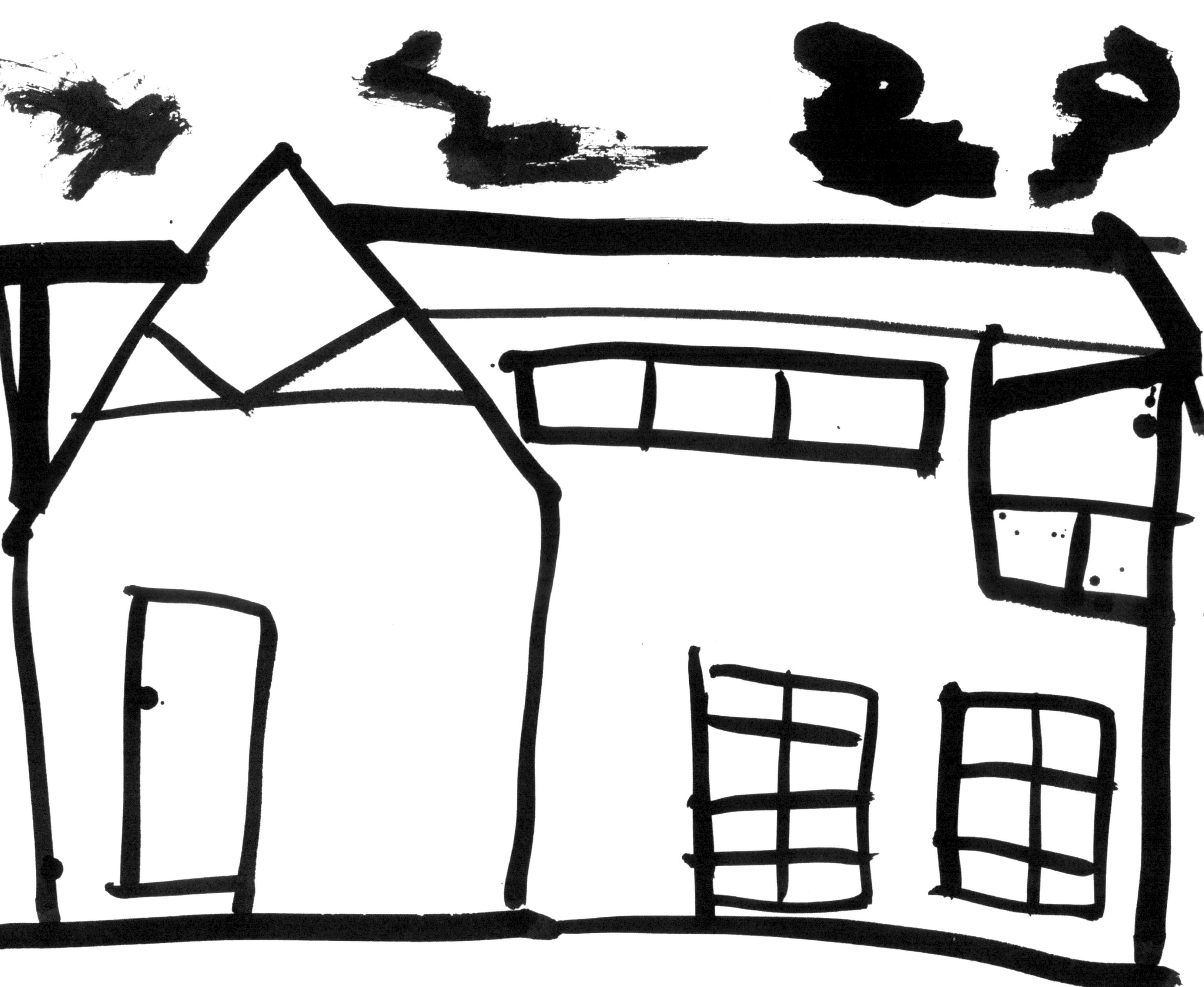

Dunes

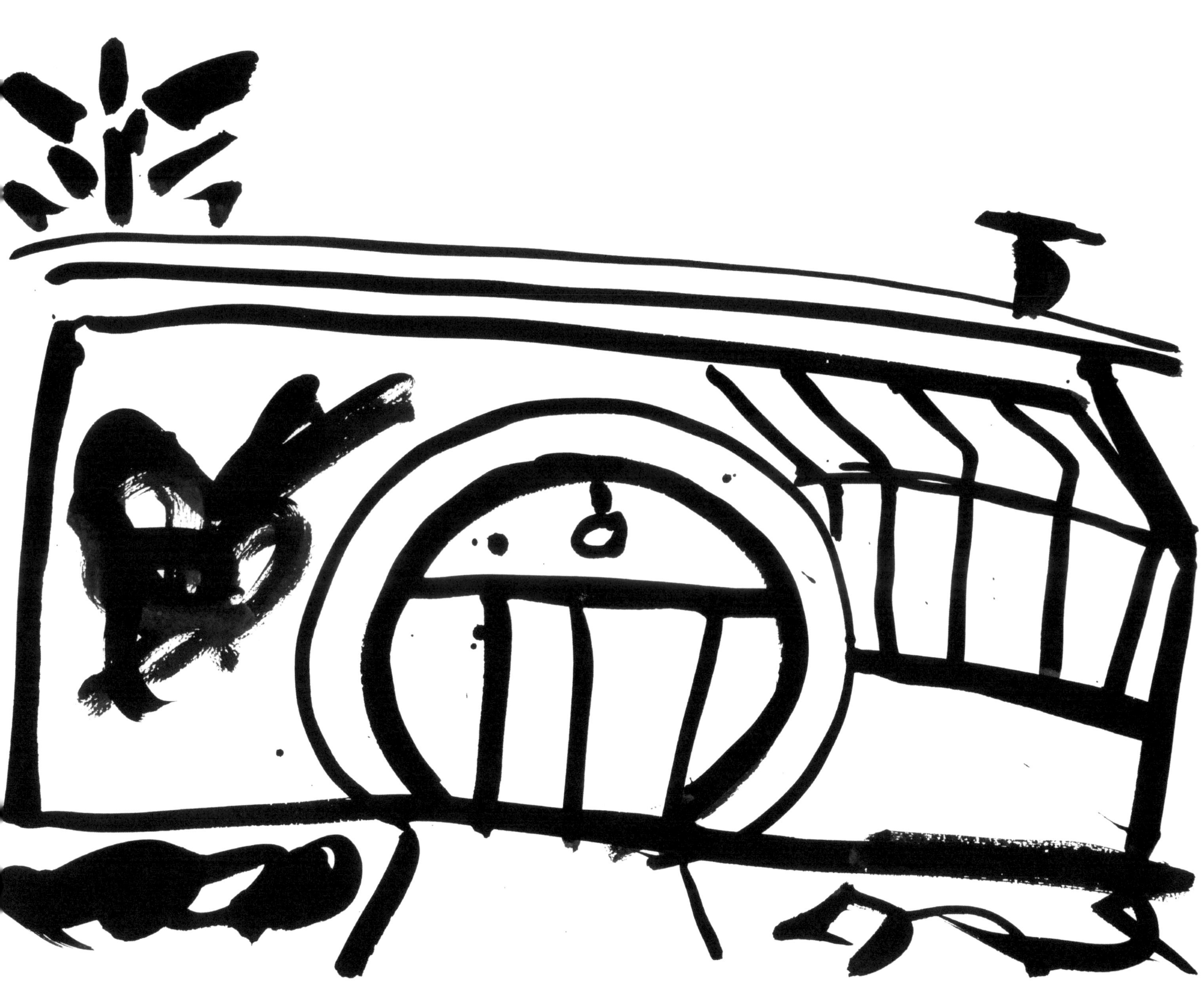

Dunes

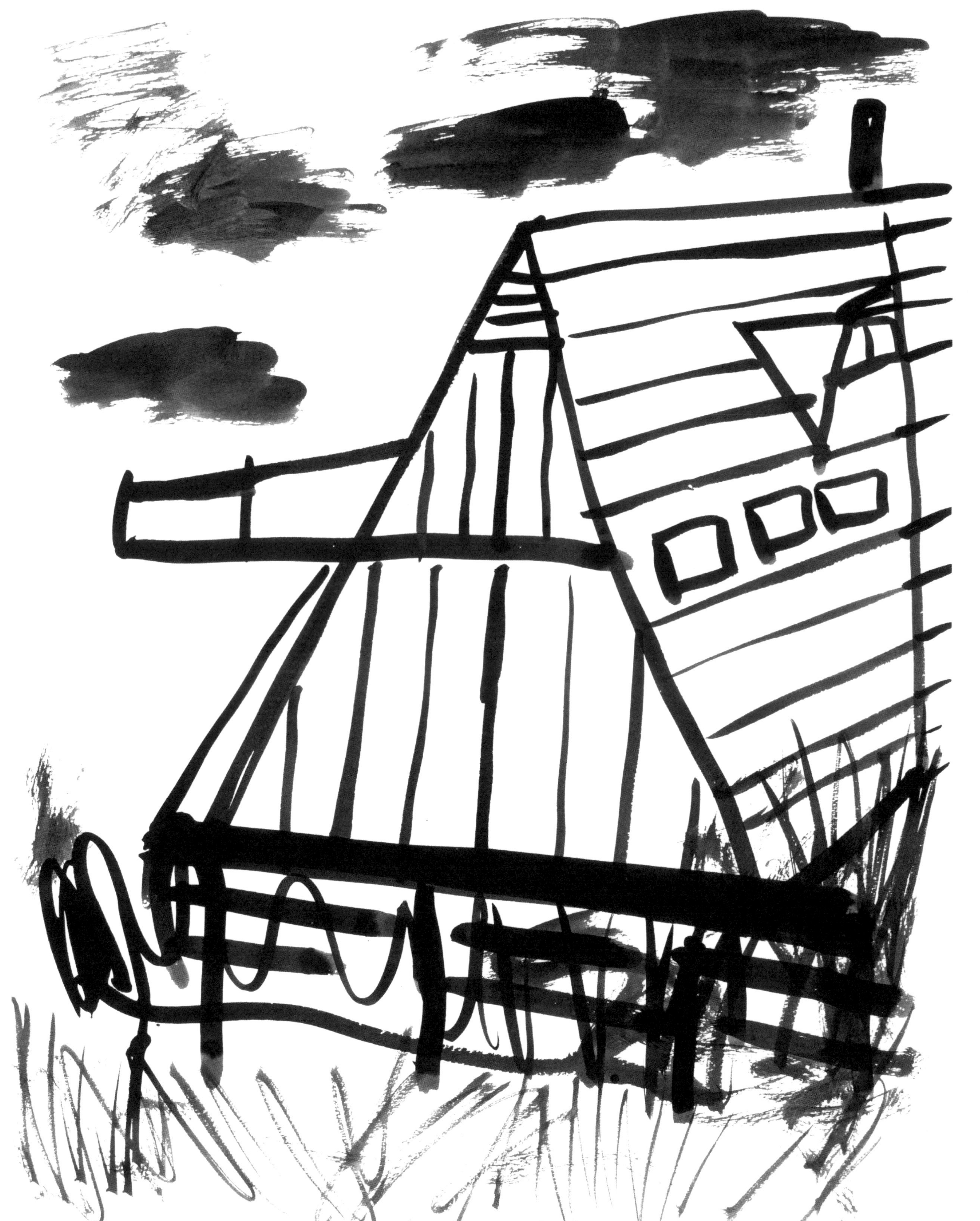

Northwest Harbor

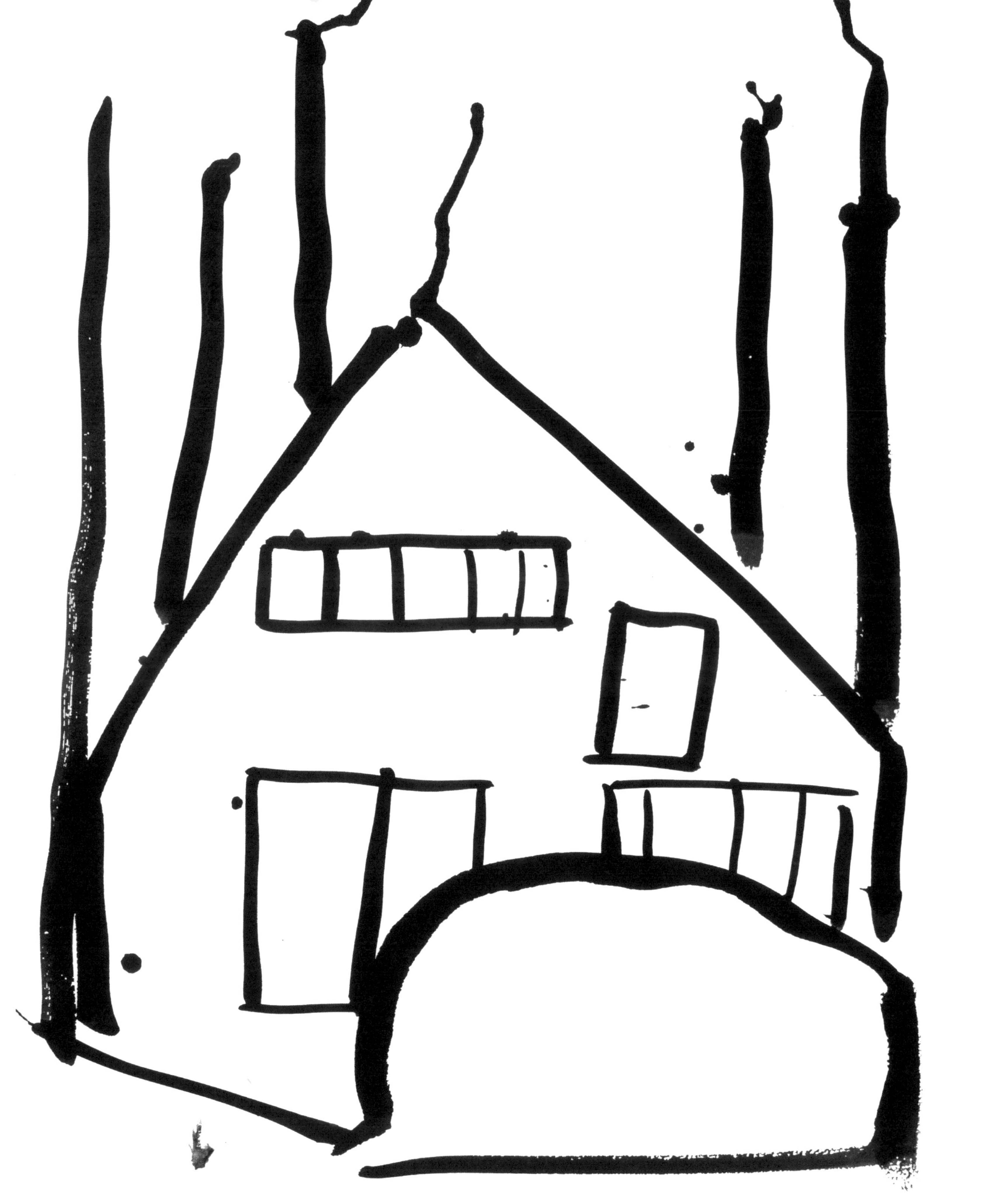

Andrew Geller, Dunes

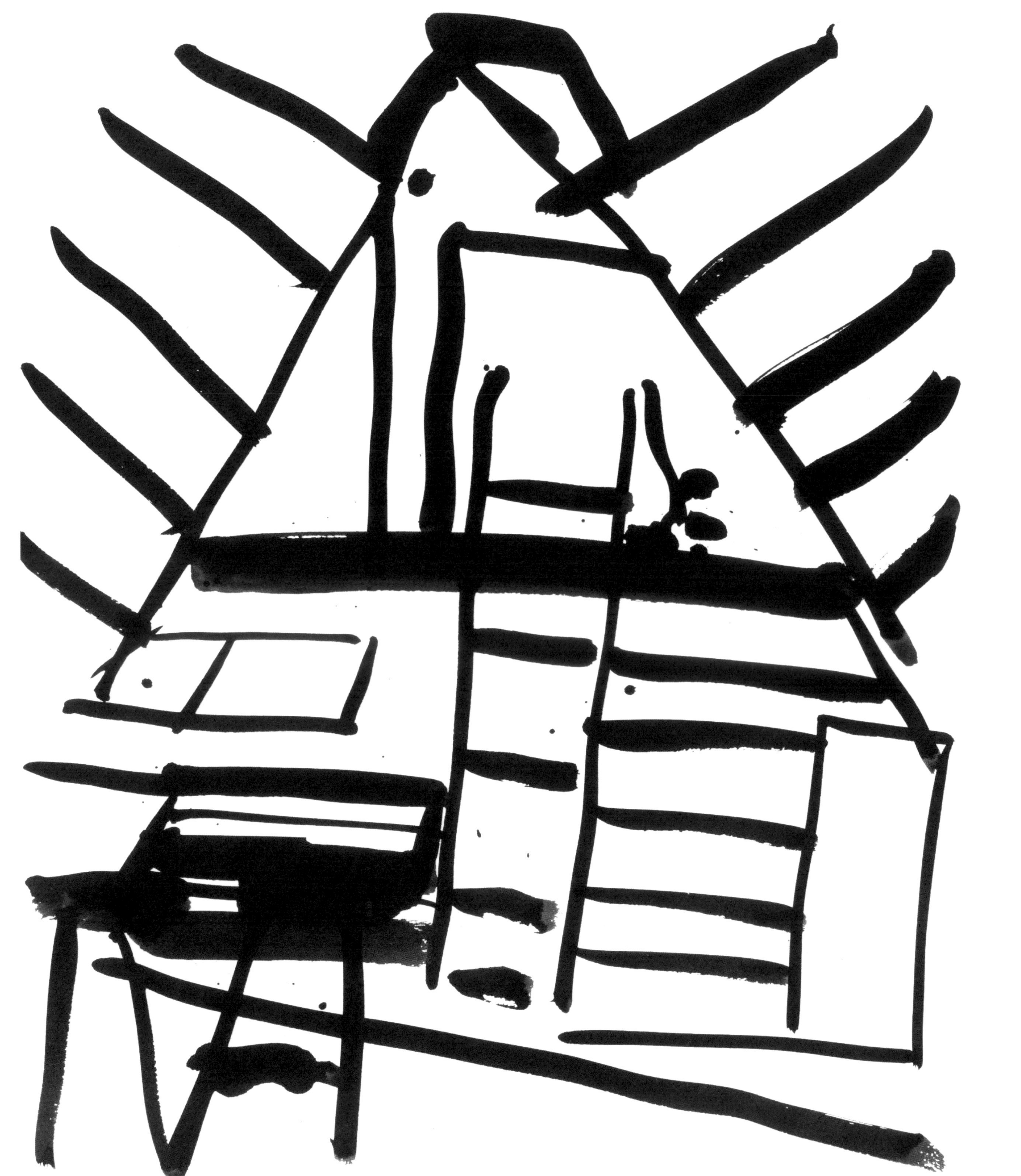

Dunes

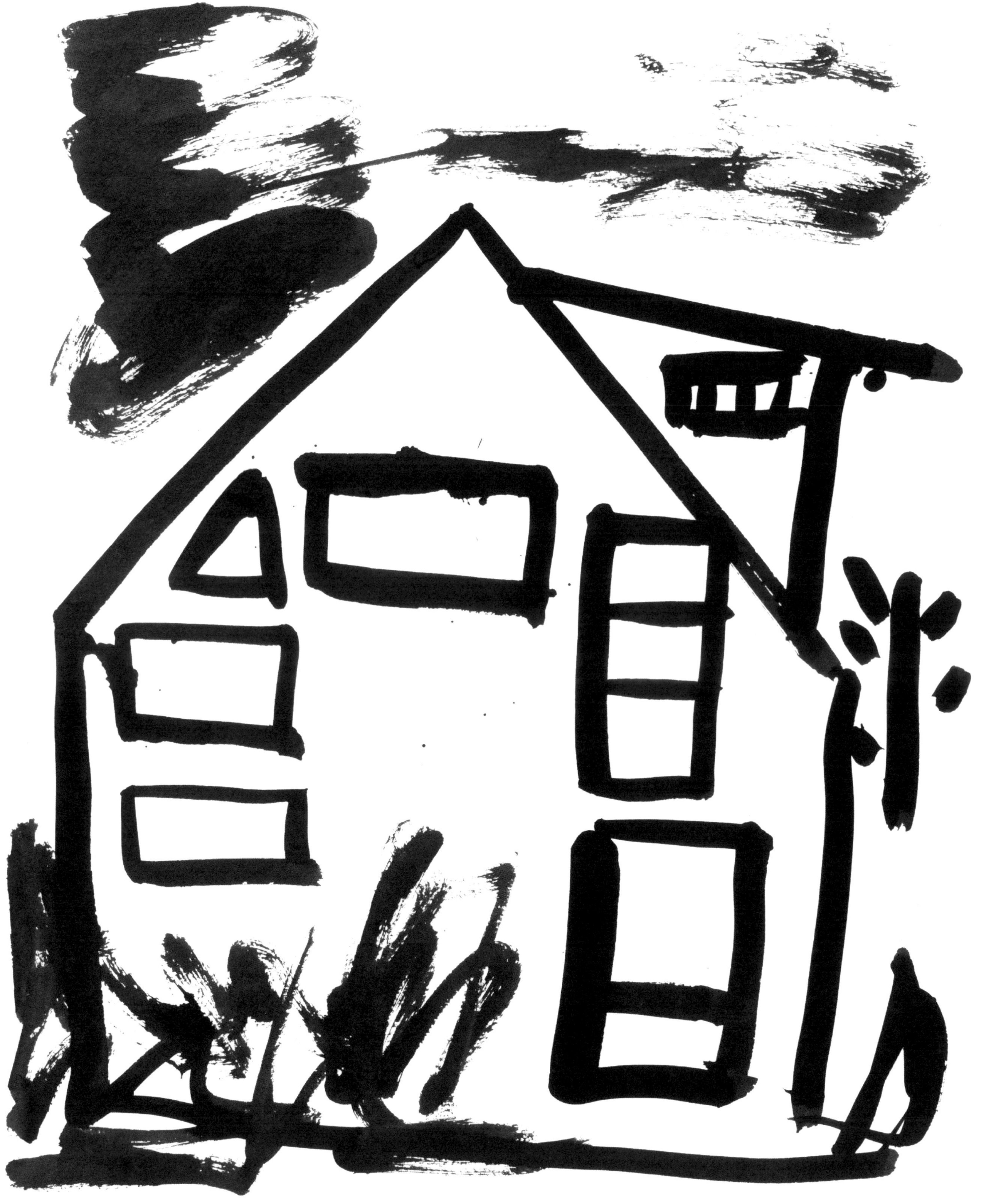

Elaine de Kooning House, Northwest Harbor

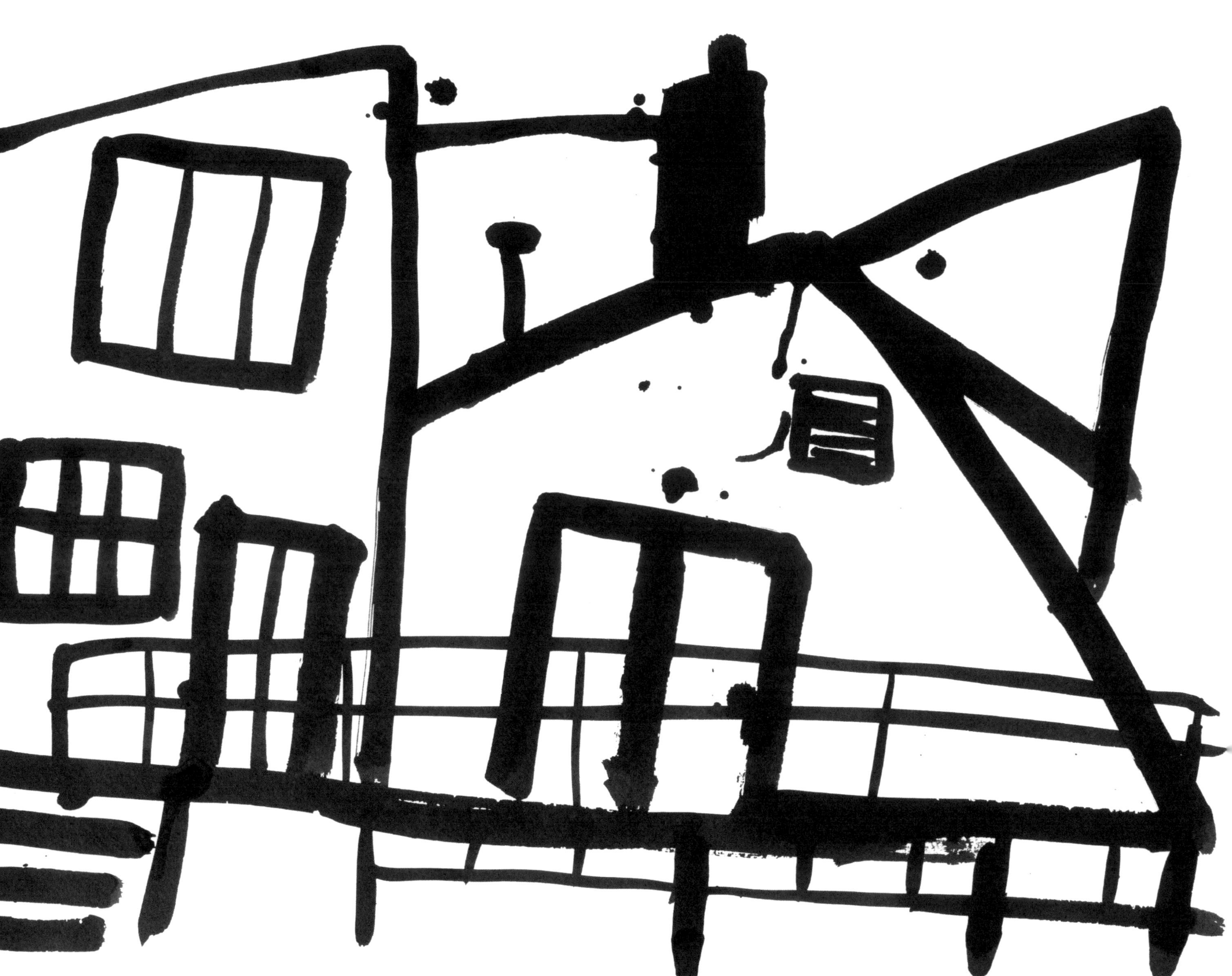

Cat House, Andrew Geller, Amagansett

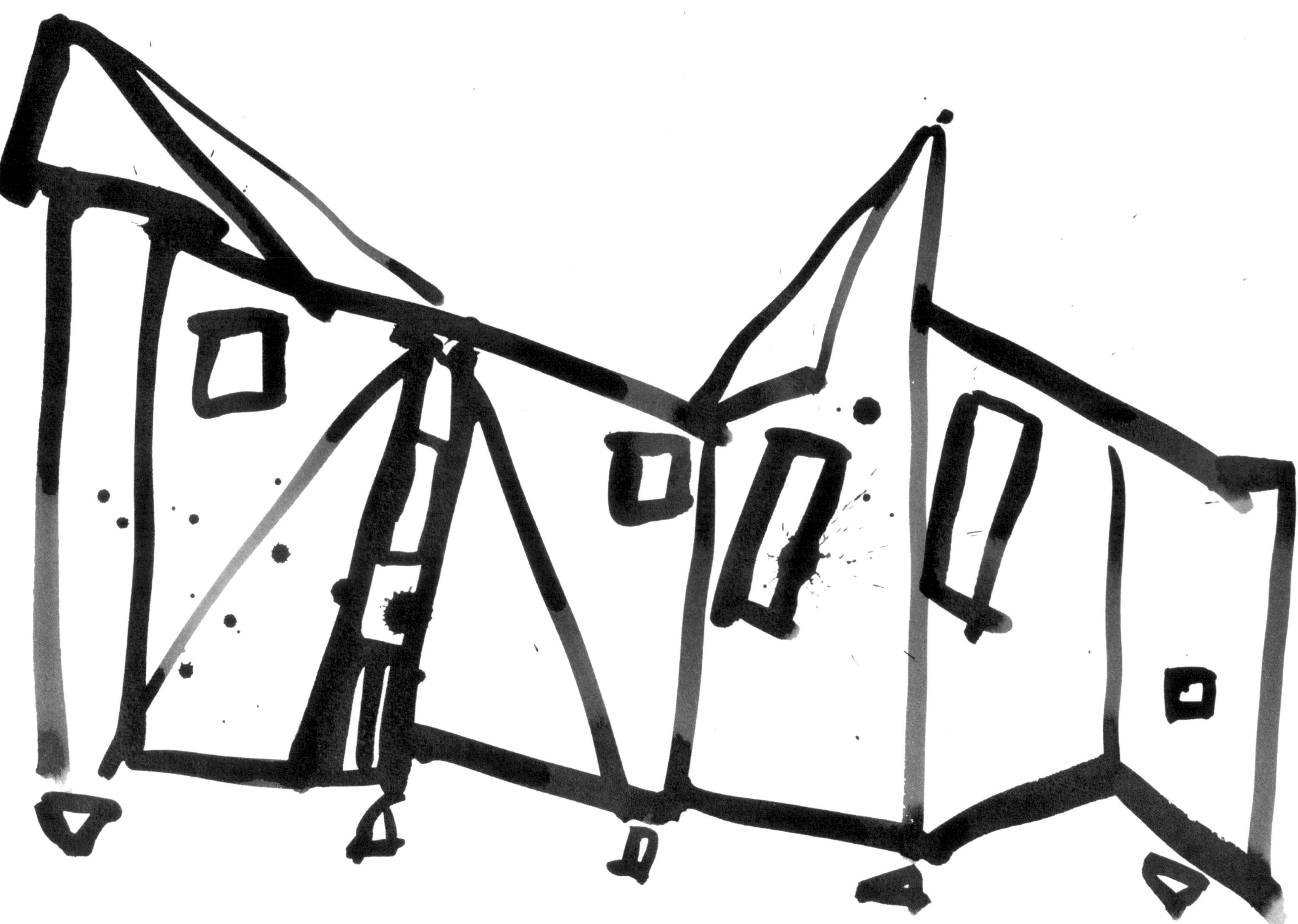

Dunes

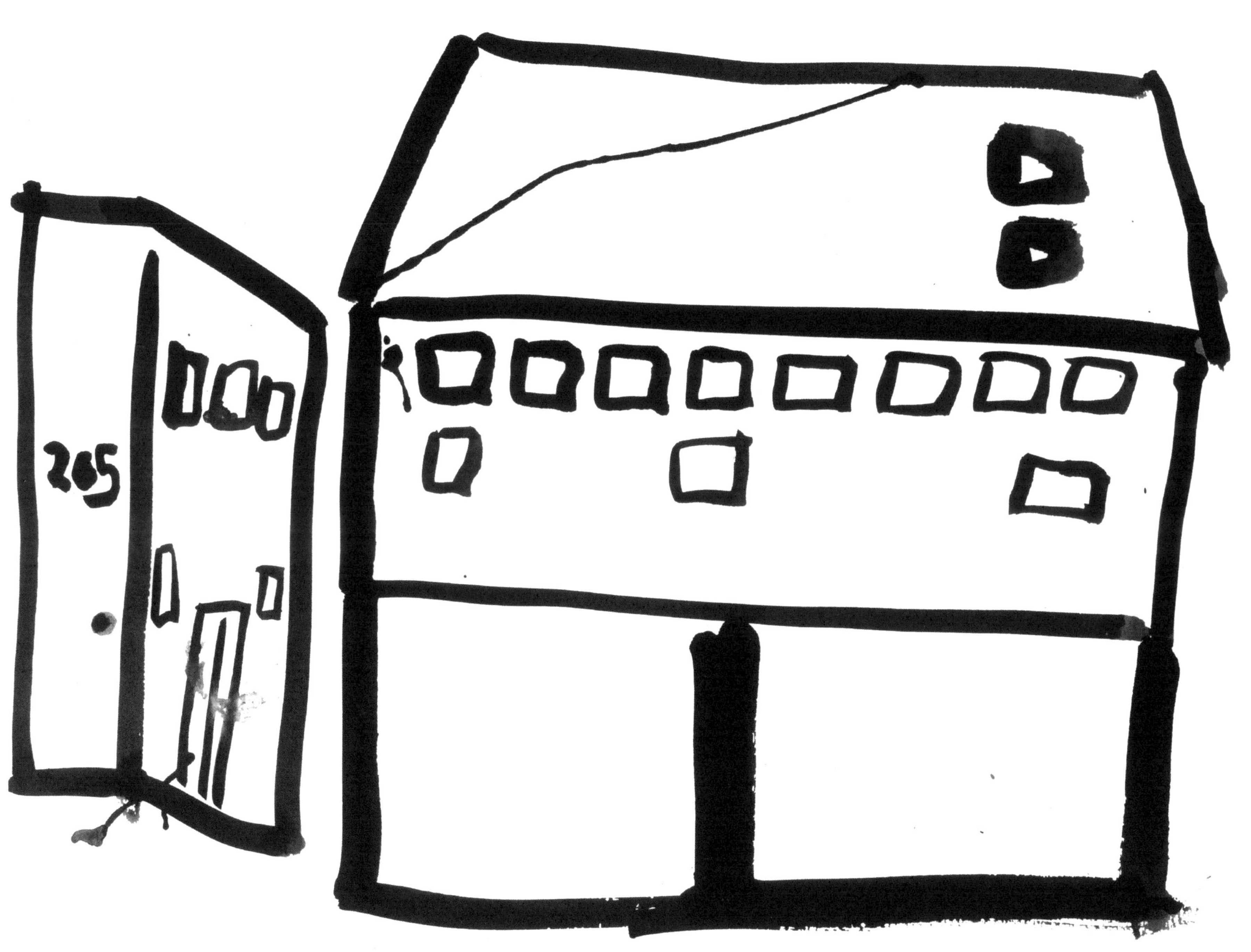
265

Andrew Geller, West Hampton

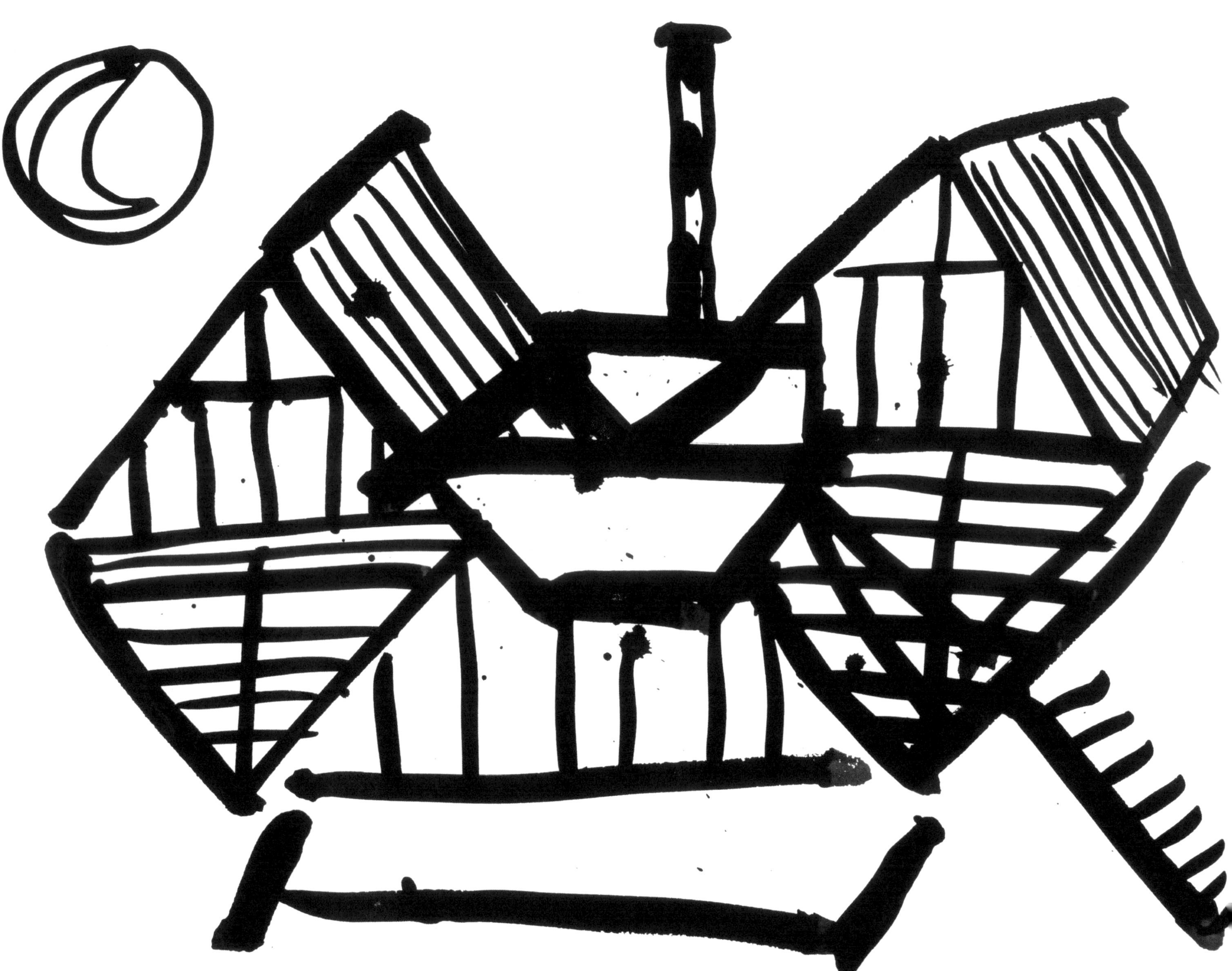

Dunes

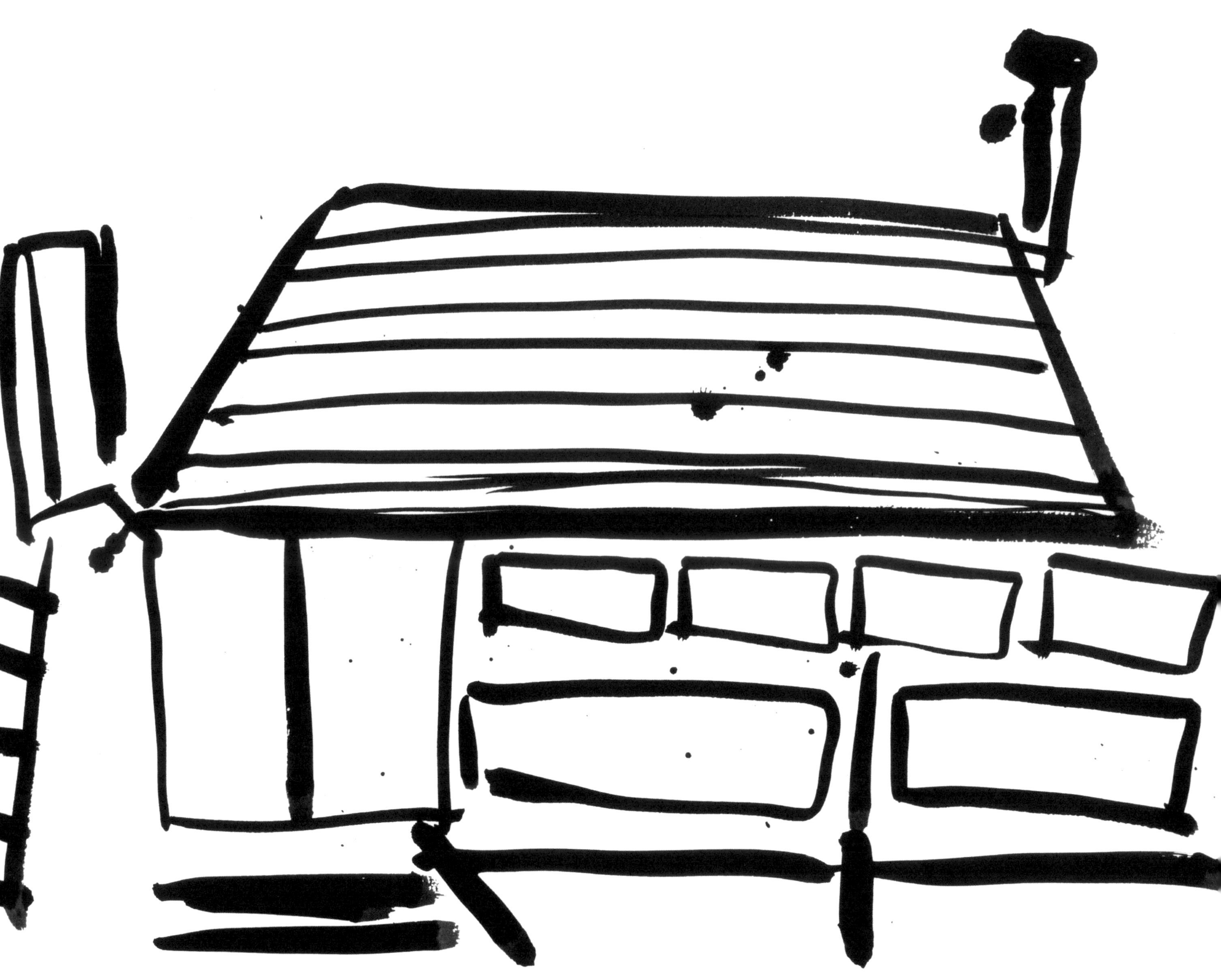

Andrew Geller, Dunes

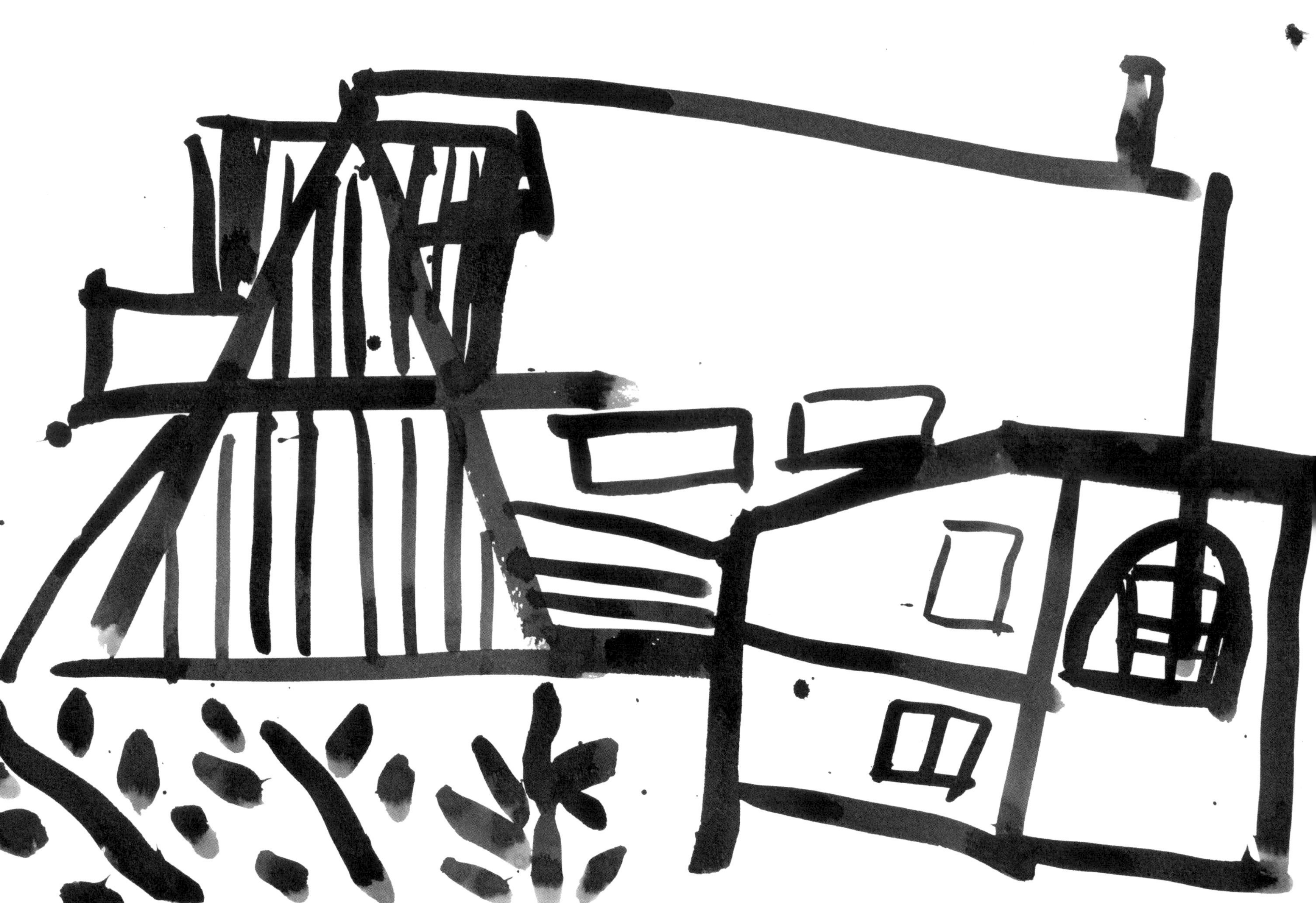

Northwest Harbor

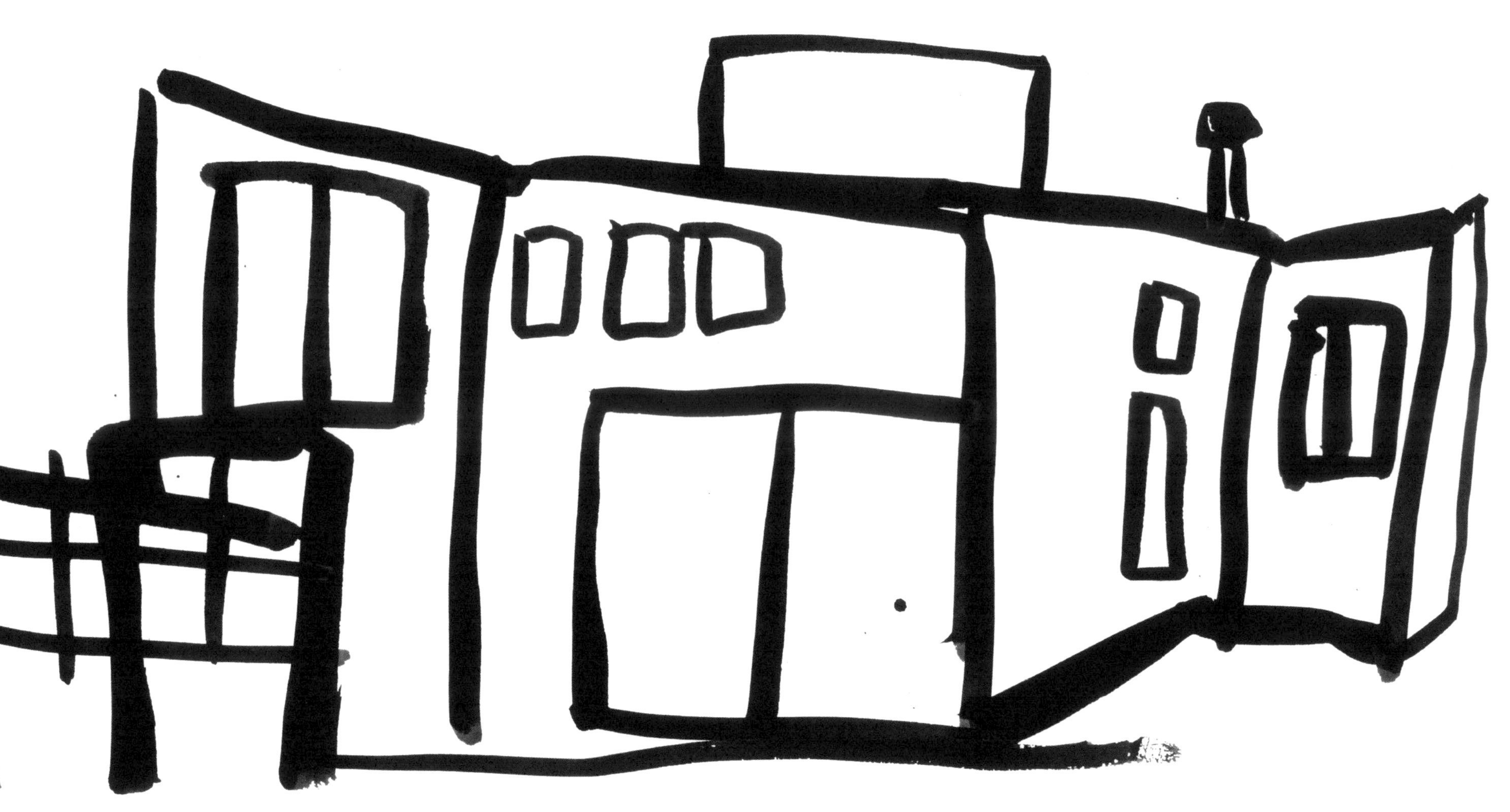

Andrew Geller, Sagaponack

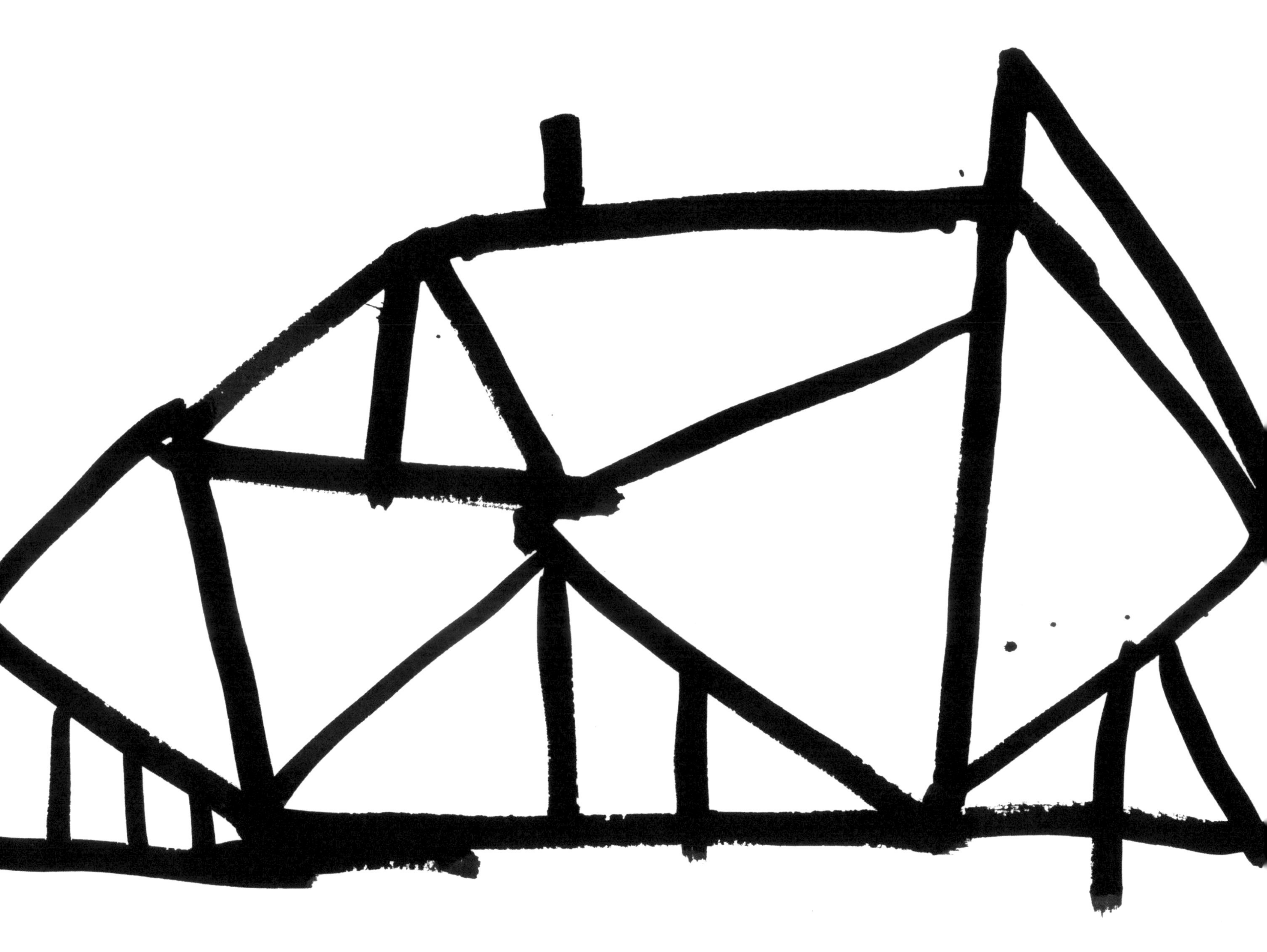

Andrew Geller, Martha's Vineyard

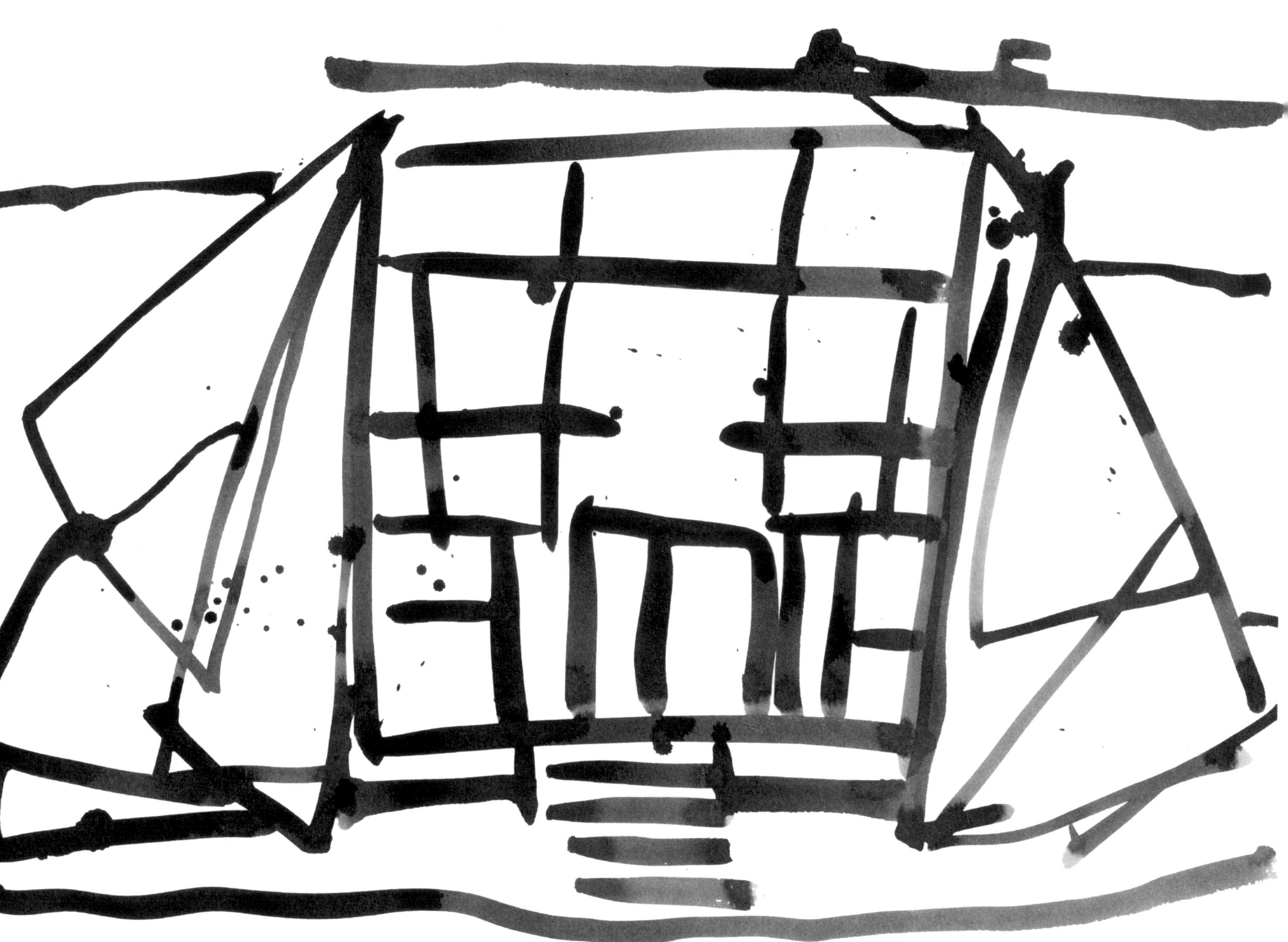

Diller Scofidio + Renfro, Amagansett

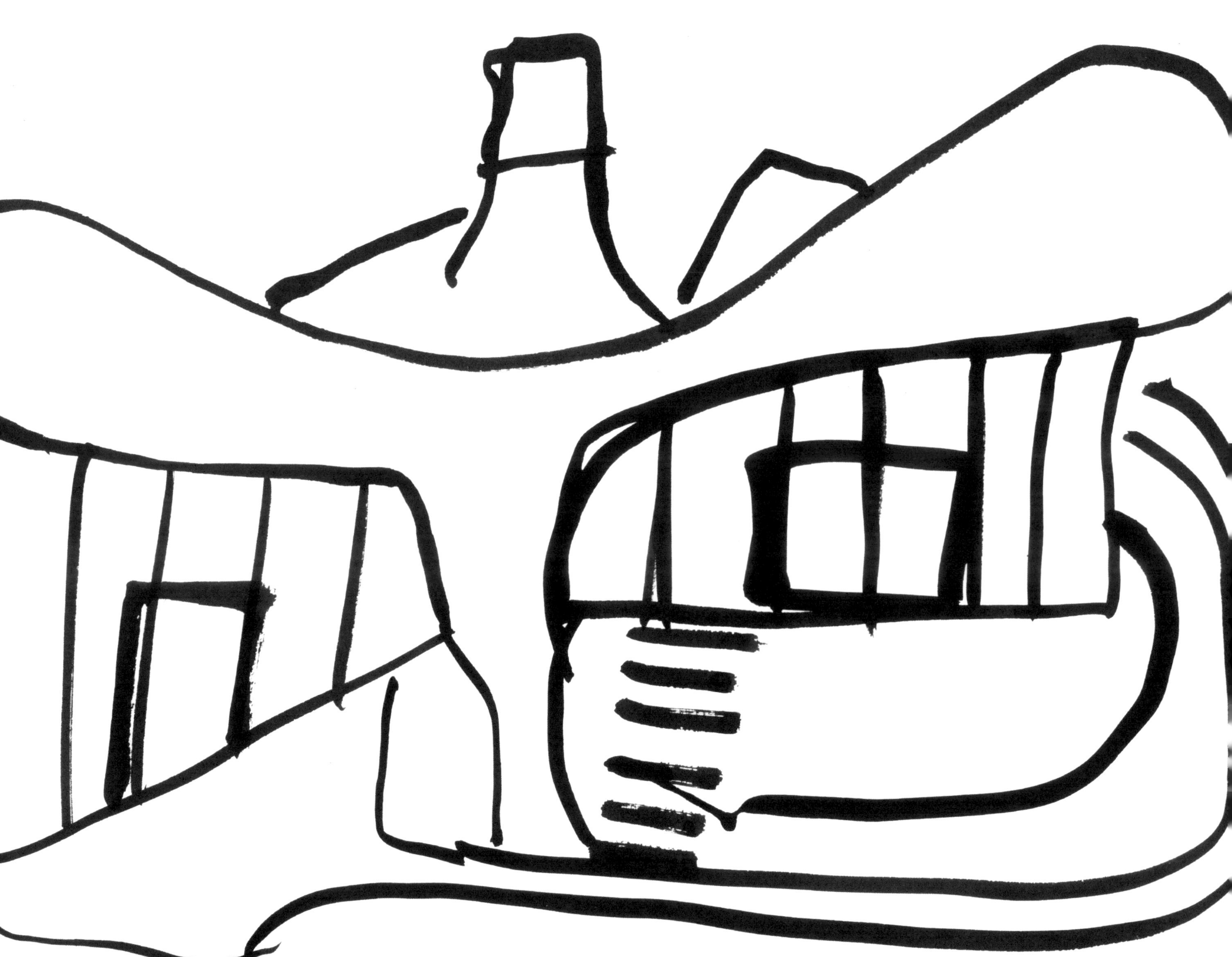

Elaine de Kooning House, Northwest Harbor

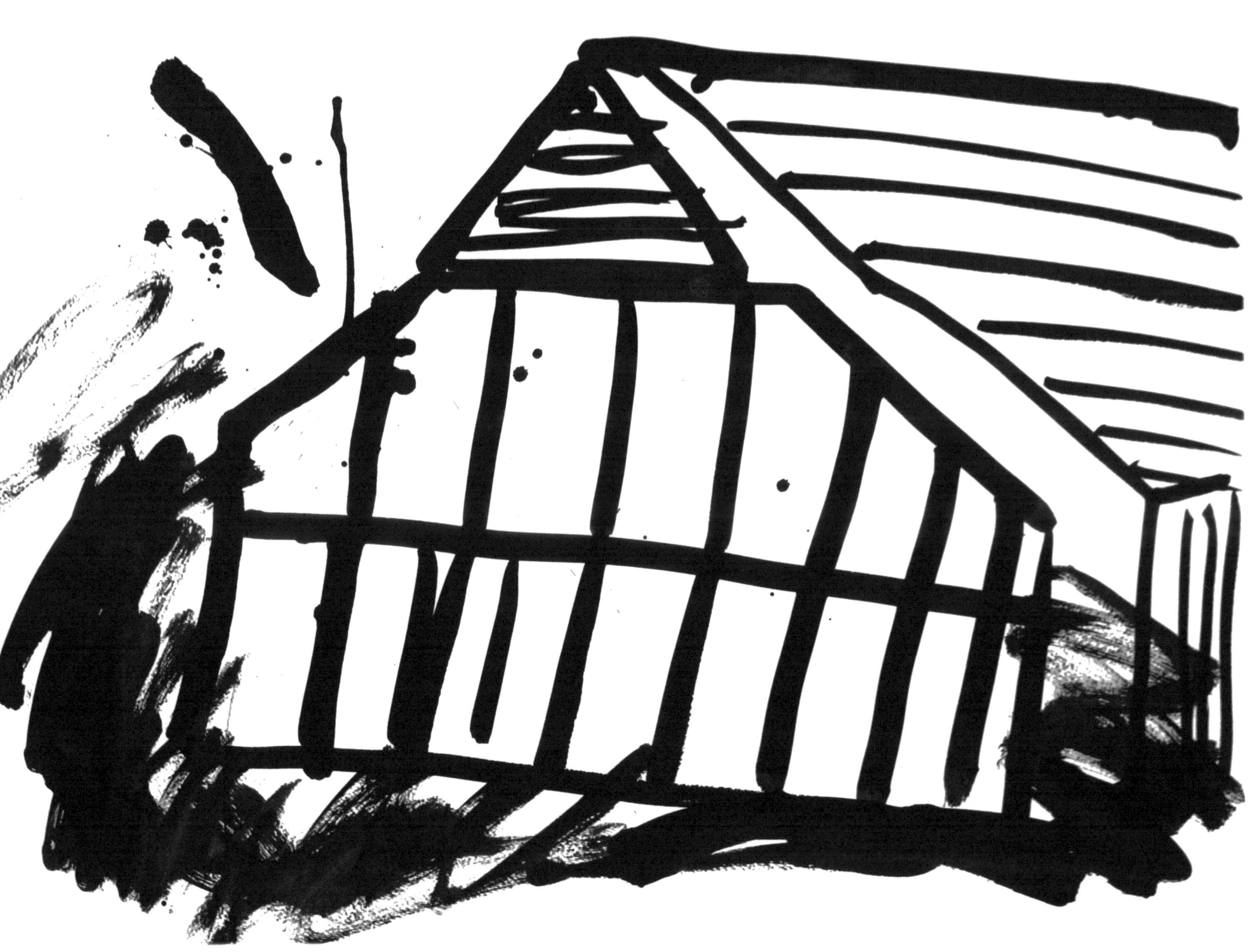

Andrew Geller, West Hampton

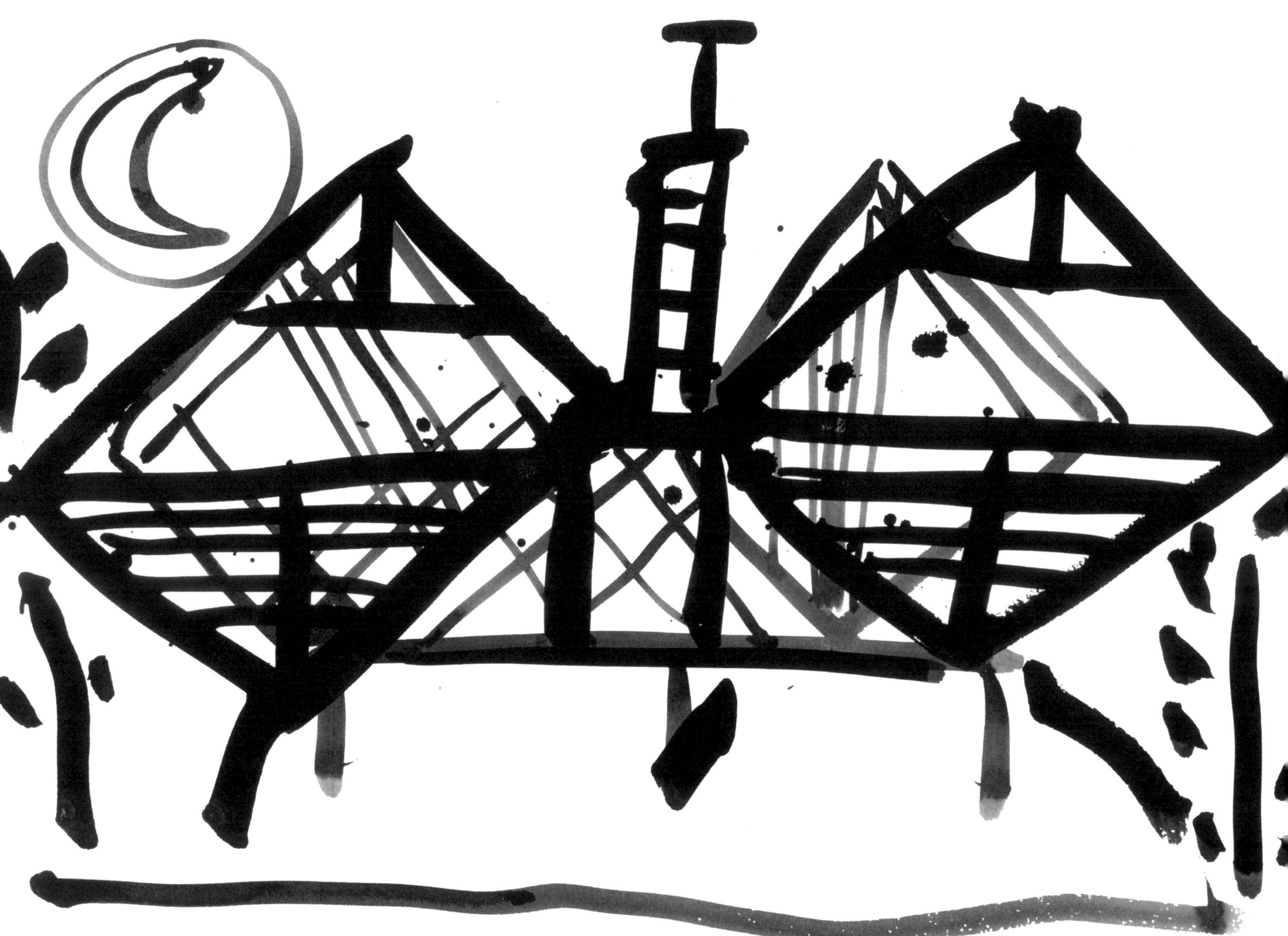

Frank House, Andrew Geller, Fire Island

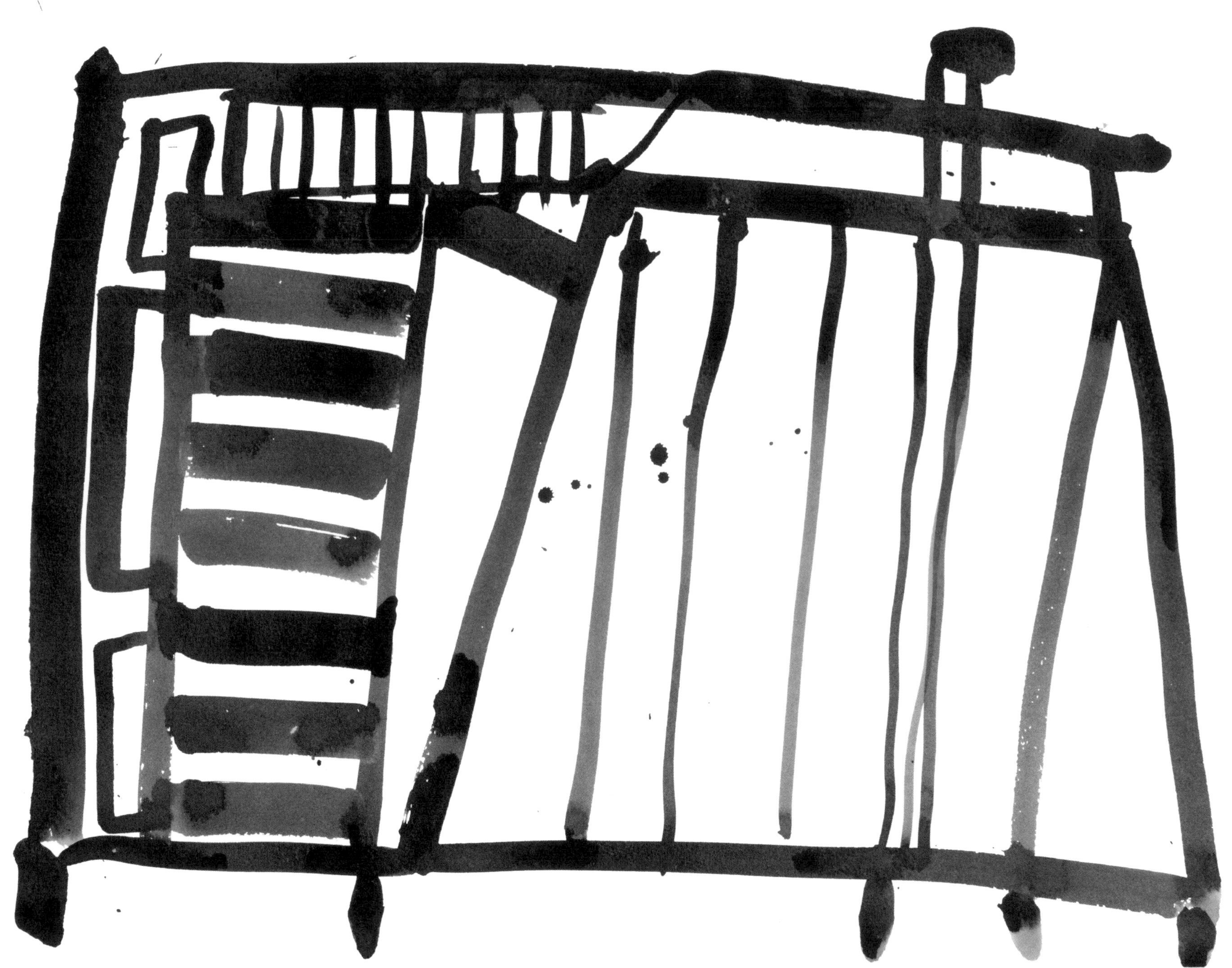

Andrew Geller, West Hampton

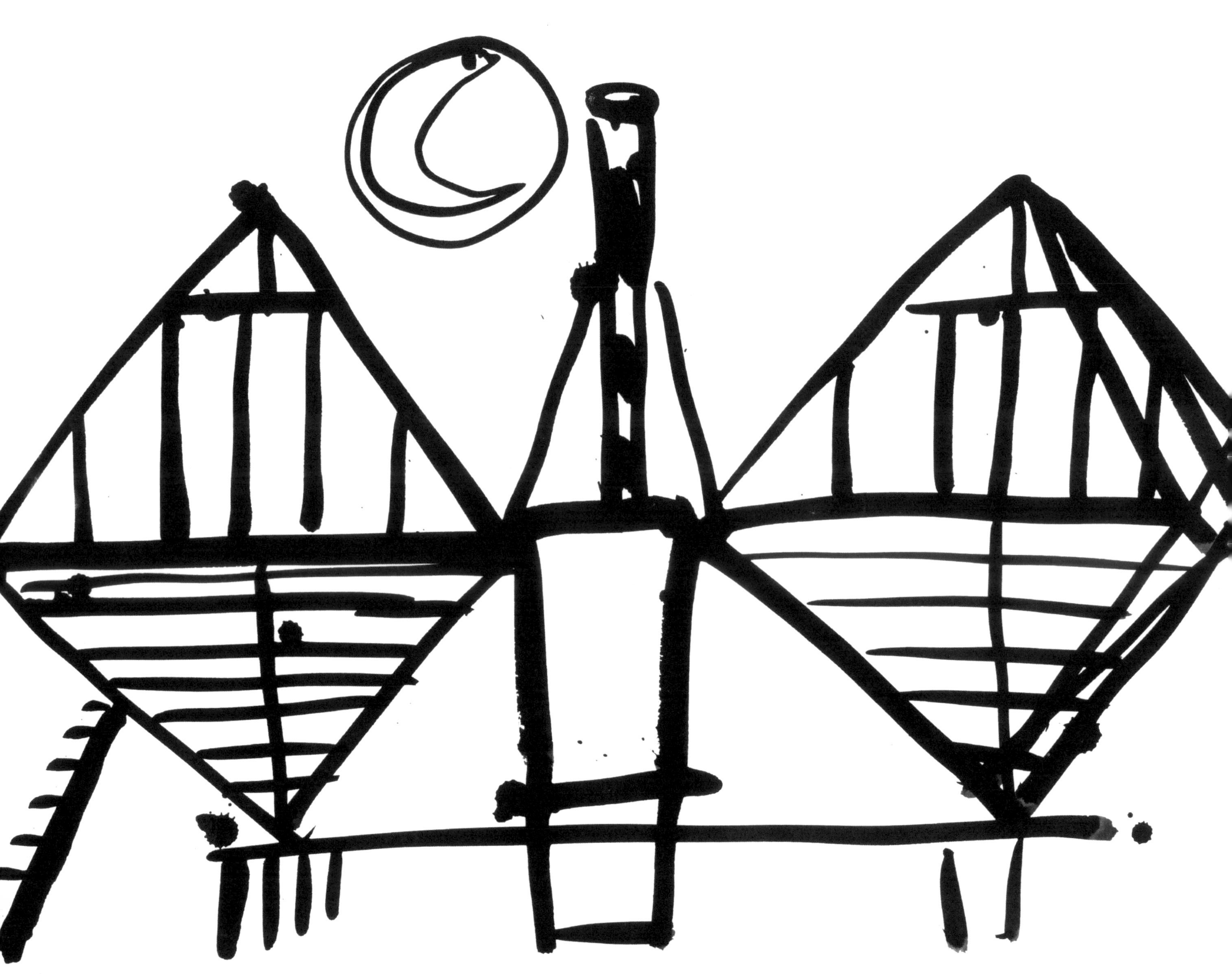

Diller Scofidio + Renfro, Amagansett

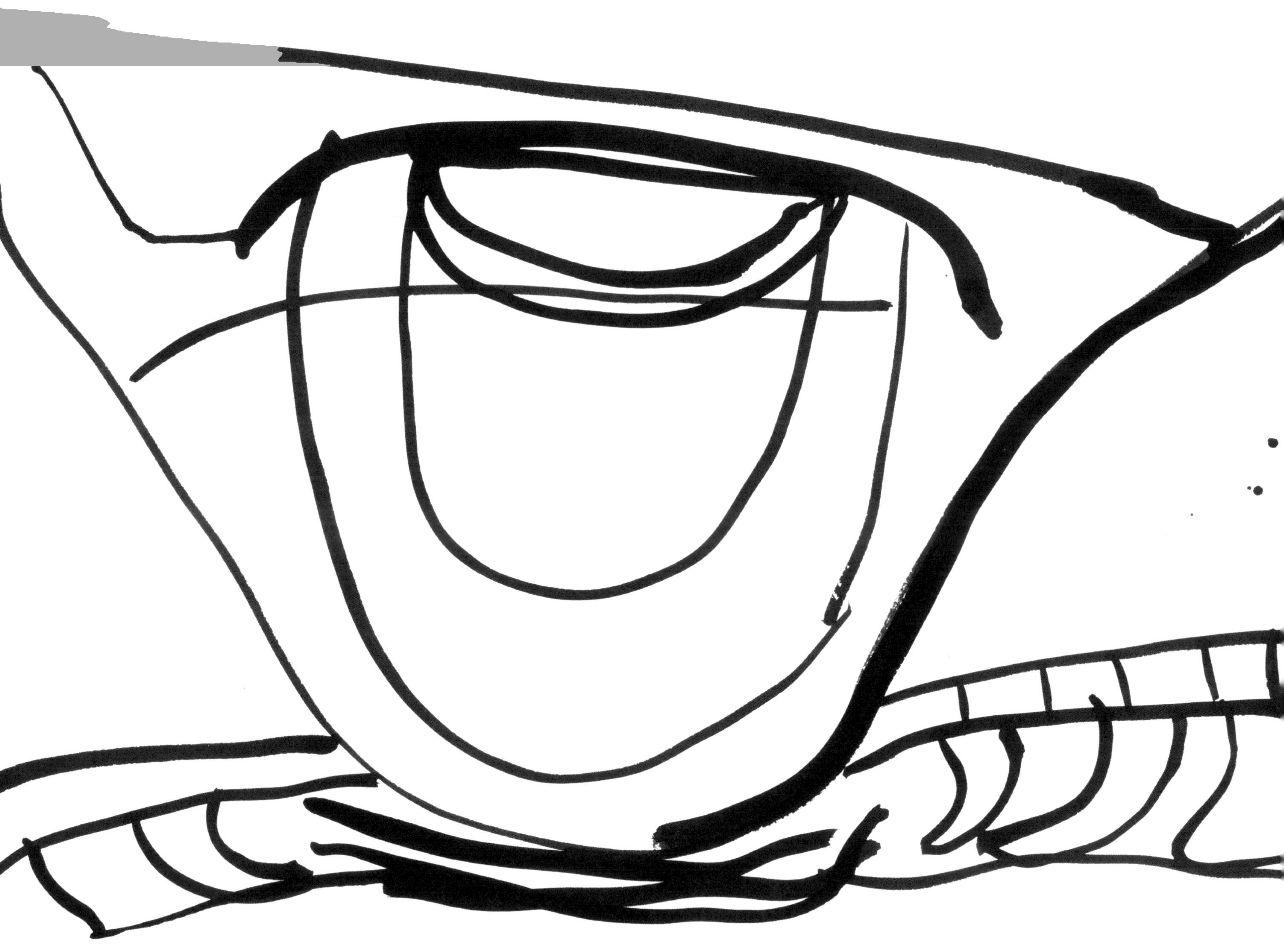

Dunes

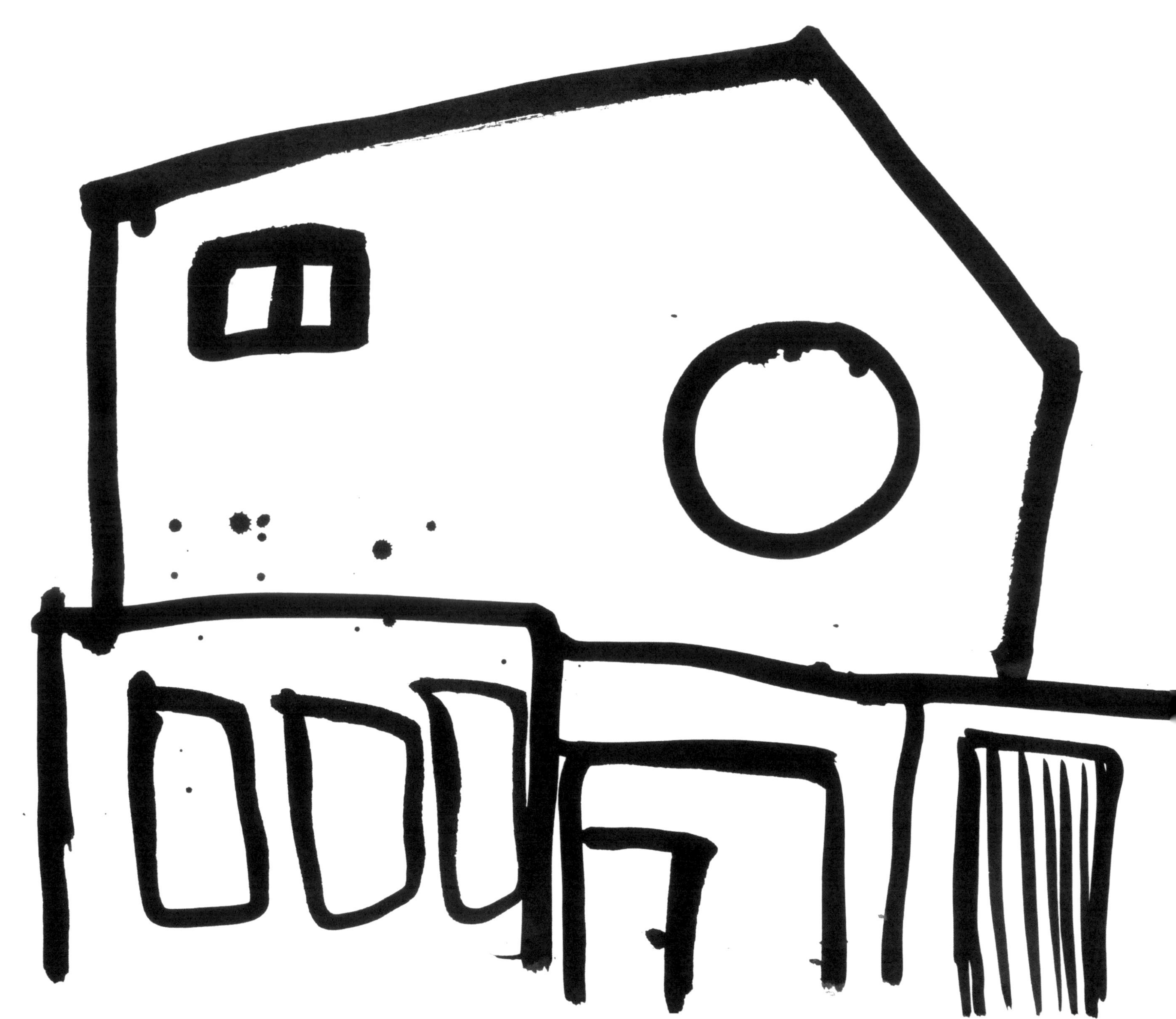

Elaine de Kooning House, Northwest Harbor

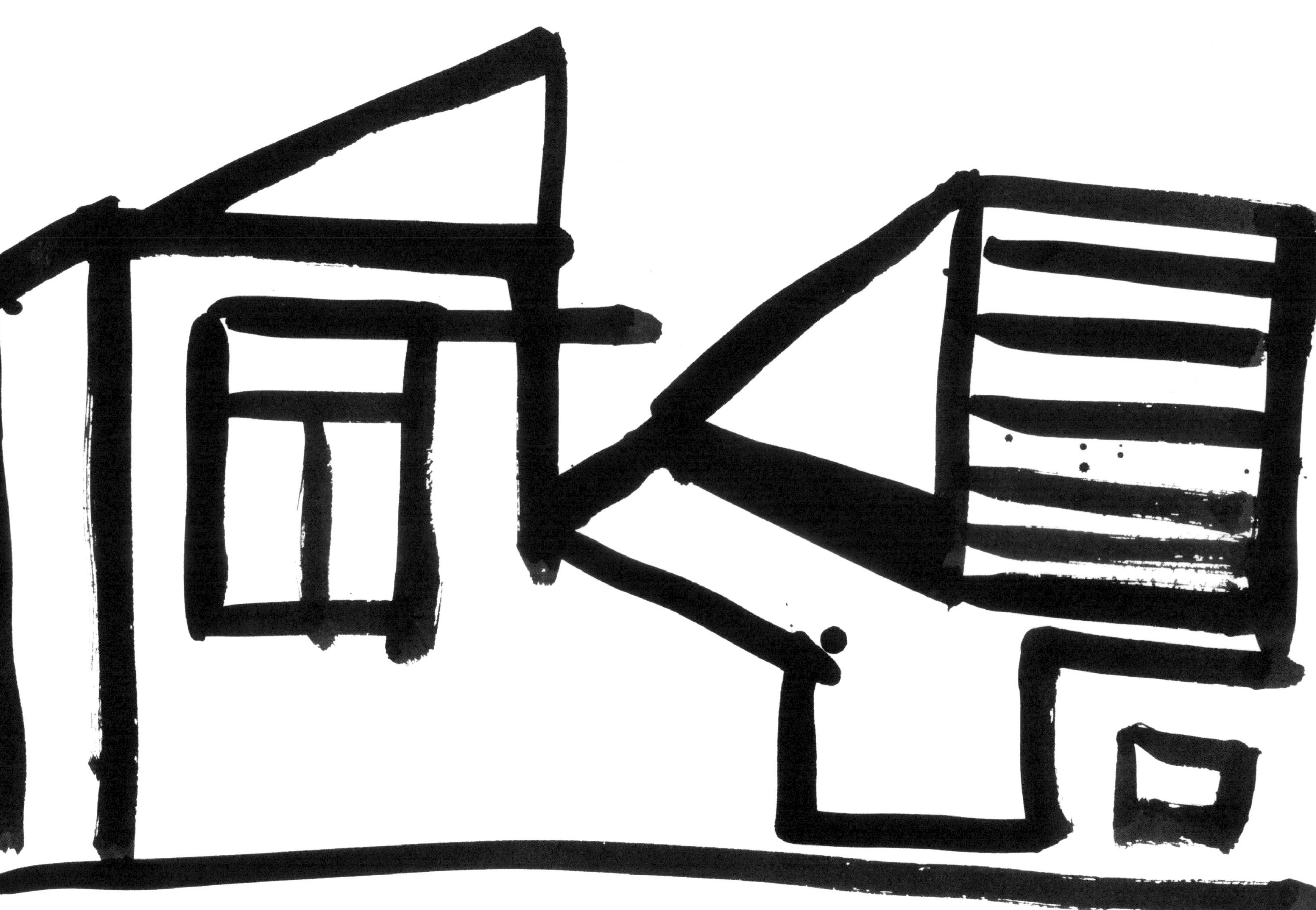

Dunes

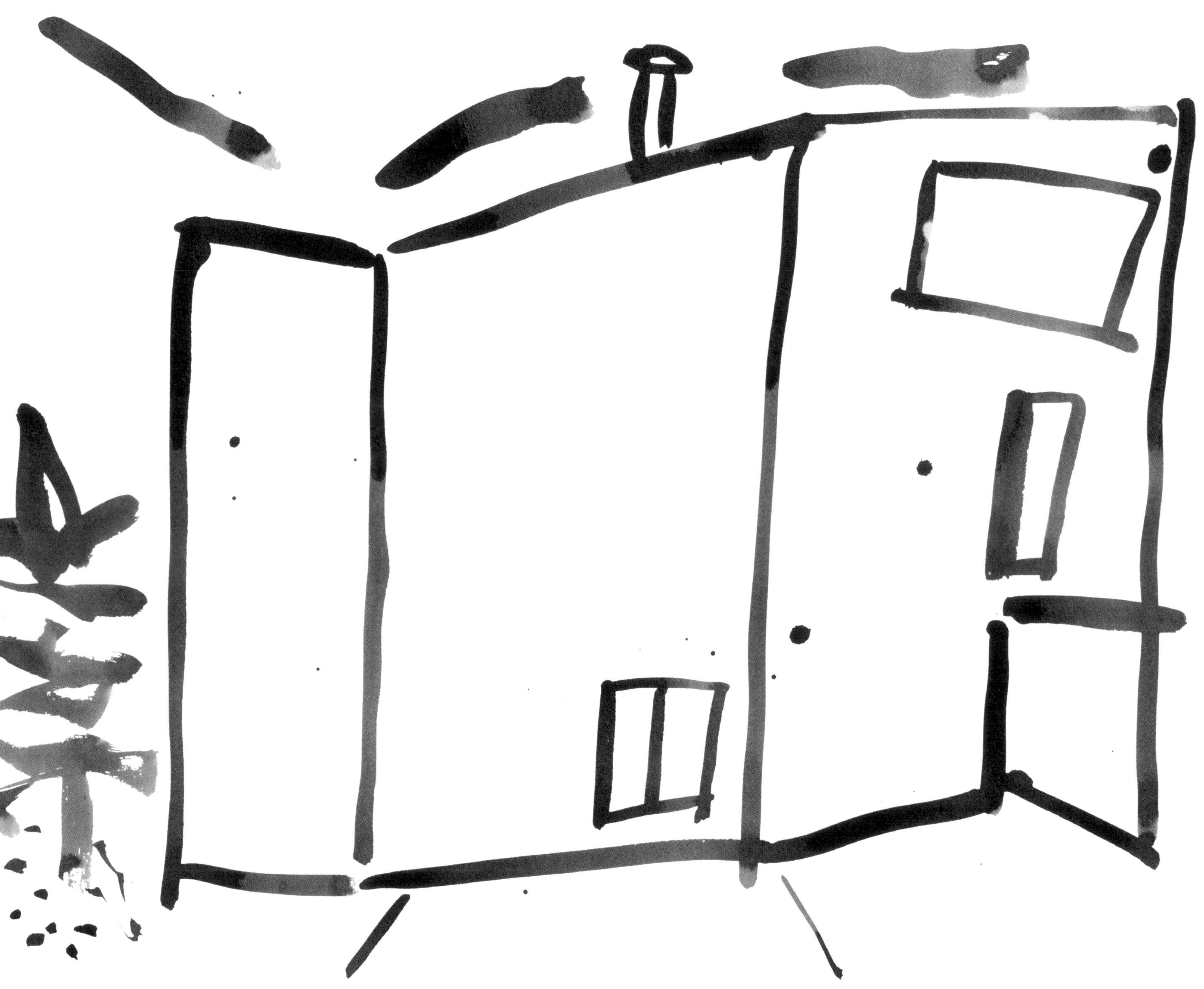

Andrew Geller, Dunes

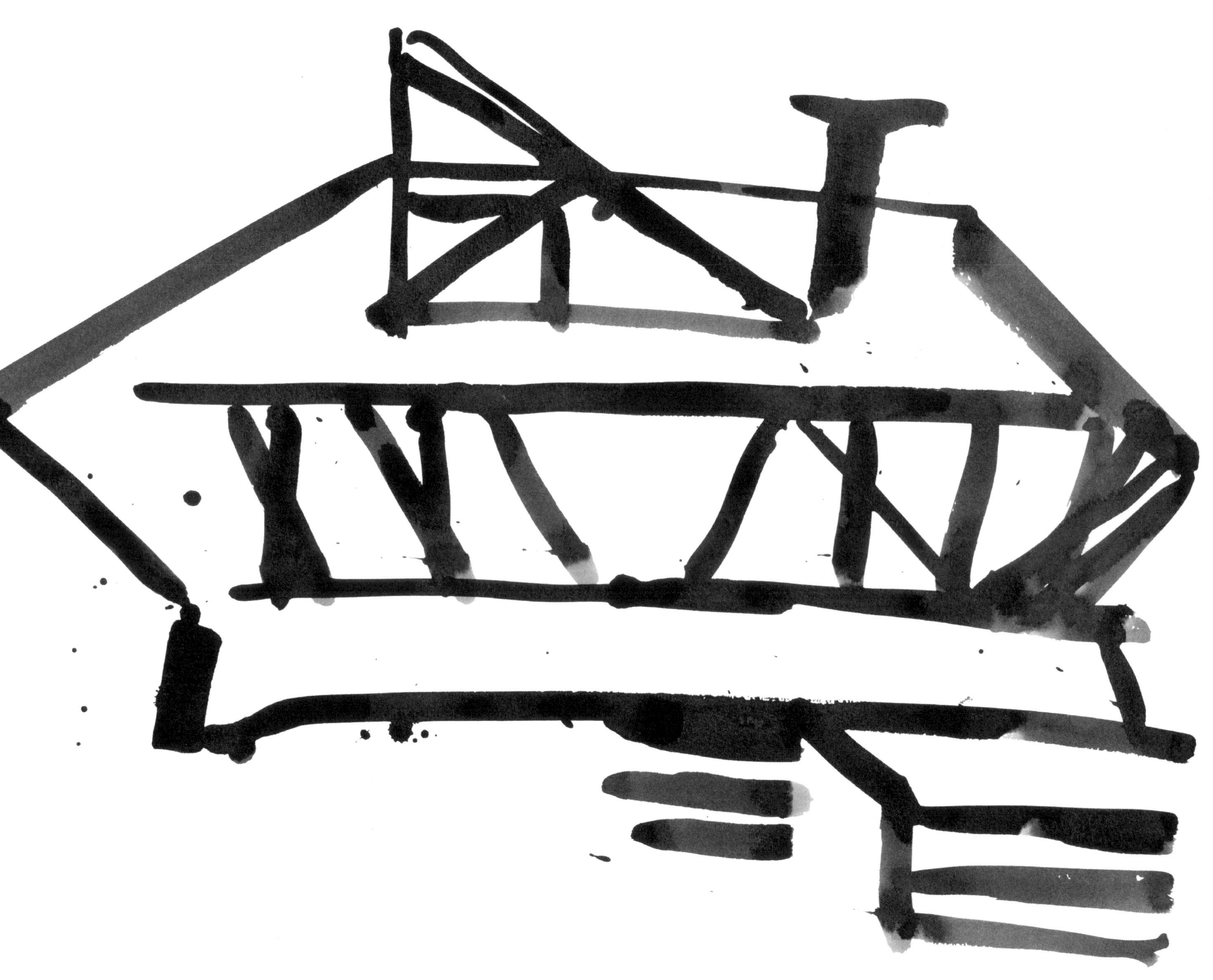

Diller Scofidio + Renfro, Amagansett

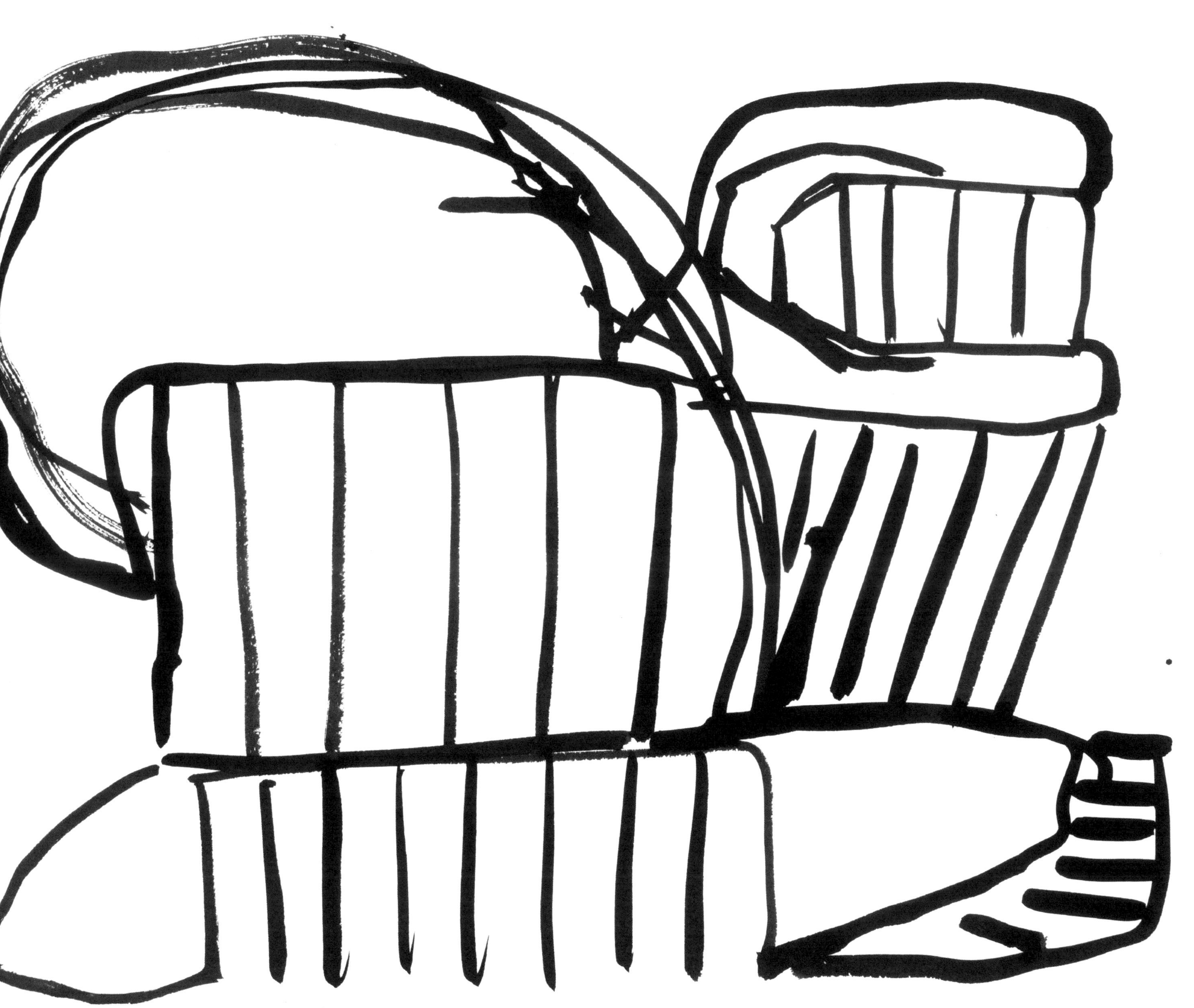

Diller Scofidio + Renfro, Amagansett

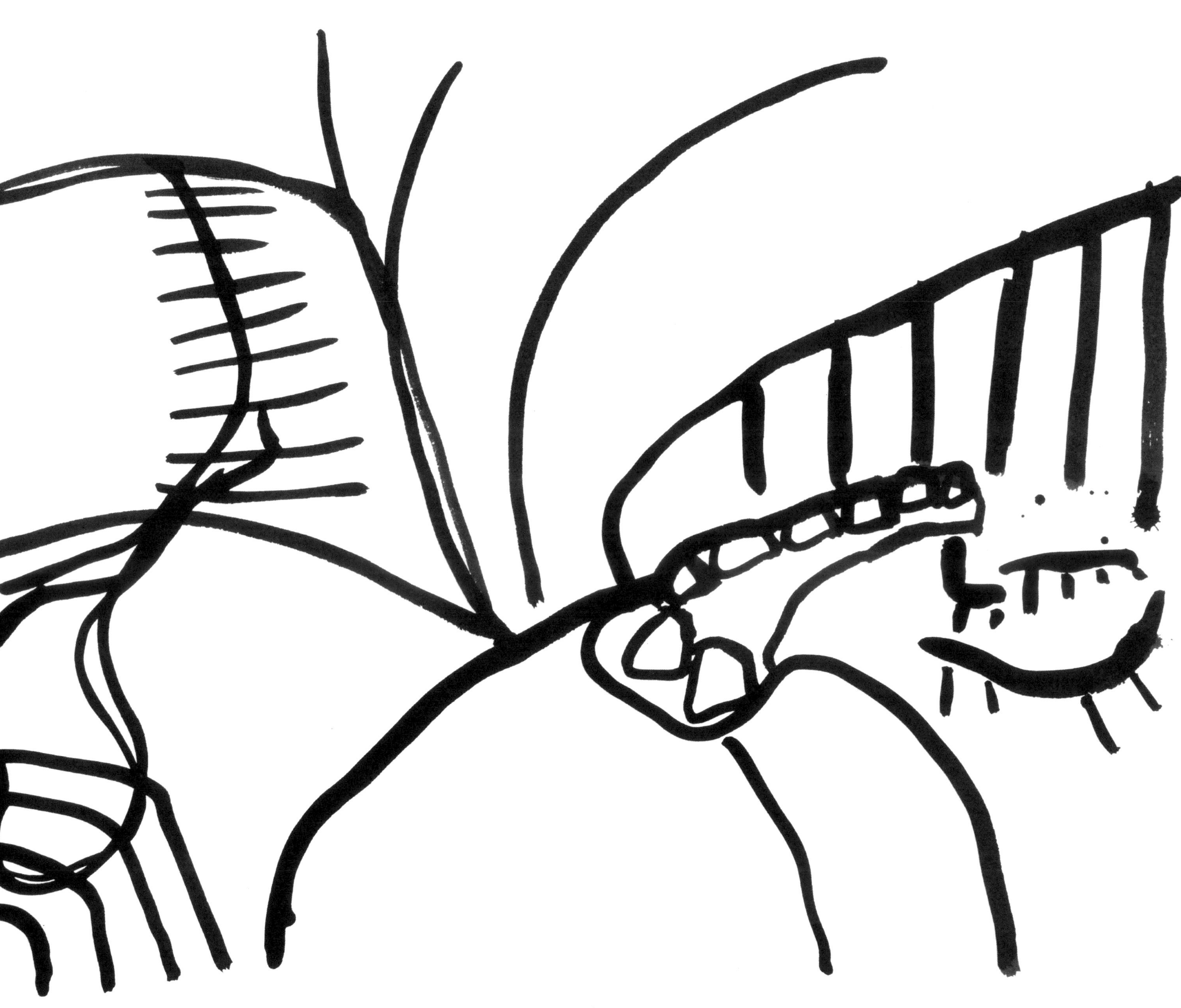

AFTERWORD

DAVID SOKOL

Long before it became internationally recognized as the pleasure garden of moneyed New Yorkers, the Hamptons was not unlike any American frontier. The Shinnecock, Montaukett, Pequot, and other peoples carefully harvested the ocean waters off Long Island for centuries prior to English settlers' arrival—and pronounced the landmass *Sewanhaka*, in honor of their ceremonial wampum. These tribes were ravaged by the establishment of colonial communities in the mid-1600s, which were ravaged by the American Revolution and War of 1812, in turn. The East End of the island was left to potato growers, a dying generation of whalers, and surviving Native Americans.

As urbanization took grittier hold of New York City after the Civil War, artists began to see the landscape's glacial dunes and modest farmhouses in a more romantic light, and they documented them en plein air. In the summer of 1878, the Hamptons' reputation as an arts destination was cemented when *Scribner's Monthly* sponsored a group of artists that included William Merritt Chase and Winslow Homer to ride the fledgling Long Island Rail Road to its terminus and pick a way to East Hampton. The magazine's freewheeling account of that adventure, "The Tile Club at Play," repositioned the area as a place to find inspiration in nature and to let off steam.

At the time of the Tile Club's outing, fine art exerted a powerful pull on the American mind. Consider the Hudson River School of painting. That art movement was born on the northern fringes of New York just a few years prior to the *Scribner's* joyride, and it fostered the nation's sense of purpose despite threats like industrialization and abolition.

The agenda of the Hamptons' artists was not nearly as grand. Here, culture entered into the service of commerce. The Tile Club flagged the Long Island's East End as an alternative summer destination for wealthy families tired of Saratoga, New York, or turned away from restricted Newport, Rhode Island. Newly established landholders built a school and subdivision around William Merritt Chase in Southampton and constructed homes and social centers nearby such as the Shinnecock Hills Golf Club. By 1893, *The New York Times* equated the Hamptons to Eden, adding, "Exclusive—in the best sense of the word—society is here represented during the summer by its choicest spirits."

While the Hamptons became a gilded playground as the nineteenth century gave way to the twentieth, its transformation did not entirely vanquish the creative community that had paved the way. In fact, the artists and architects left standing persevered in innovation. Chase ruled Southampton's Art Village until 1902; legendary architect Stanford White effectively codified the Shingle Style in the clubhouse design at Shinnecock; William Muschenheim launched his architecture career with a set of Bauhaus-inspired structures in Hampton Bays; impressionist Frederick Childe Hassam flourished at Willow Bend in East Hampton until his death in 1935.

By slowing the gentrification of the Hamptons, the Great Depression and World War II made room for a new generation of arts pioneers to put down roots. Jackson Pollock and Lee Krasner arrived in East Hampton in 1945, purchasing a house in the hamlet of Springs, and the couple would be followed in short order by Mark Rothko, Willem de Kooning, and Theodoros Stamos. Some artists employed existing houses as residences and studios while others patronized a new architecture that strove to be as unfettered, and perhaps shocking, as the artwork itself. Around 1944, Robert Motherwell tapped French architect Pierre Chareau to adapt two government-surplus Quonset huts into his East Hampton base, and Peter Blake turned the conventional house plan upside-down for Gucki Mulally in Montauk in 1961. The Hamptons was poised to become the artist colony that should have manifested decades prior. Or at least its bohemian element promised to exist relatively peacefully alongside the local elite, who were gaining exposure to action painting and abstract expressionism at places like Guild Hall and the Signa Gallery.

Yet the frisson of status and creativity, or of nature and artifice, was no secret. *The New York*

Times and *Life* magazine regularly covered the Hamptons in its pages, and the publicity captured the imaginations of New York's emerging professionals. Emboldened by a postwar culture of individualism and disposable income, a new order of people descended upon the Hamptons, and the region became a laboratory for a new type of residence—the second home.

To be sure, the East End already sported plenty of weekend and summer residences. For the social elite, these houses often combined references to English country manors and the architecture of Long Island's long-gone whaling industry, or they recreated an owner's preferred travel destination. For the creative elite, the buildings were more academic than spectacular, meditating over modernist history or maximizing workspace. Leisure housing for the middle class, on the other hand, demanded accessibility in both financial and intellectual terms. The architect Andrew Geller was poised to fulfill that need.

In 1955 Geller had been an employee of the famed industrial designer Raymond Loewy when the firm's public relations director, Elizabeth Reese, tapped Geller to design a weekend home in Sagaponack. For an extraordinarily affordable $7,000, the architect produced an A-frame house perched high atop a dune that sported smart, irreverent touches like a cantilevered walkway, white-painted cross bracing, a fireplace flanked by windows, and an upper-story bedroom accessible only by retractable ladder. Ever savvy, Reese had her new escape published in the *Times*, and Geller's freelance career took off.

Geller did not say much, officially, about modernist orthodoxy, but gladly defied it. Early on, he made variations on the A-frame theme by rotating a rectilinear volume on its axis or tapering it like a Mayan temple; then he moved on to develop forms inspired by origami and canvas sails. Throughout, his buildings thumbed their noses at the architectural establishment, and at social convention generally. In cedar shingles and plain-sawn lumber, Geller's designs encapsulated the collision of artistic daring, economic mobility, and popular optimism uniquely taking place in the Hamptons. And they simultaneously honored the waterfront landscape that had convened all these forces in this far-off corner of Long Island in the first place. The achievement undoubtedly nourished architects Horace Gifford and Harry Bates, who were peers of Geller in both age and geography, and it provided fodder for Geller's successors to build upon or react to.

This fascinating, intersectional moment in history—and Geller's almost innate ability to give it three-dimensional form—has resonated with Katherine Bernhardt. The artist's calligraphic drawings and photographs of Geller's and others' Hamptons houses are rendered with buoyancy, and the subjects of her gaze are unanimously playful, even irreverent. While much of the Hamptons' mid-century heritage has been lost to weather and redevelopment, Bernhardt's images prove that the spirit of Geller and his era persist and delight to this day.